ÁGOTA KRISTÓF
COLLECTED PLAYS

Ágota Kristóf

COLLECTED PLAYS

Translated by Bart Smet

OBERON BOOKS
LONDON

WWW.OBERONBOOKS.COM

First published in the English language in 2018 by Oberon Books Ltd
521 Caledonian Road, London N7 9RH
Tel: +44 (0) 20 7607 3637 / Fax: +44 (0) 20 7607 3629
e-mail: info@oberonbooks.com
www.oberonbooks.com

A catalogue record for this book is available from the British Library.

PB ISBN: 9781786820747
E ISBN: 9781786820754

Cover design by Ricky Simmonds

Contents

Introduction

*'I read. It is like a disease. I read everything that comes
to hand, everything that meets my glance: [...]
I am four years old. The war has just begun.'*

Ágota Kristóf was born in 1935 in Csikvánd, Hungary a
small village on the Austrian-Hungarian border. From
very early on she reads and reads. A possessive pastime
that was only moderately encouraged, mostly frowned upon.

Alongside her 'reading disease' grows this other 'disease':
telling stories, making things up, inventing stories that would
start *one sentence, any sentence, and then ..., and then ...*
There is no end to the story.
She felt no need to write at the time. There was no need. That
only came later, when *'the silver thread of childhood'* was severed.
Writing as a cure for the pain of separation.

At the age of fourteen, she enters a boarding school with a
strict regime, hard straw mattresses and meagre food. Separated
from her two brothers and parents, she starts writing in a big
notebook, in an invented language to keep her thoughts, dreams
and fears safe from others. There she wrote her first poems, poems
she would later describe as too poetic, too sentimental. She also
wrote short sketches that she and her classmates performed in
the dorms, to the delight of pupils and teachers alike.

1956. The Russians invade Hungary. On the night of the
27 November that year, Ágota Kristóf, twenty-one years old,
married for two years with a four-month-old daughter, followed
her husband over the border, reluctantly leaving behind her war-
torn homeland. Her husband held their baby in his arms. She
was carrying two bags, one with diapers, food and clean clothes
for the baby, the other holding dictionaries.

They end up in Neuchâtel, Switzerland, a small village. Life
has to start all over again. Again there was the pain of separation,
separation of her family, her books, her writing, her village and
country.

Now she found herself in a country whose language she did not speak or understand. Continuing to write in Hungarian felt impossible, as impossible as learning that new language, French. Long slow years passed before she got to grips with French and started to write again. Not poetry, neither did she write stories or longer prose; she started again by writing plays.

John and Joe, her first performed play, was well received, installing in her a sense that becoming a writer was possible after all.

She continued writing for the stage. Other plays were performed. Some of these scripts were broadcast on Swiss radio, earning her her first royalties. Today her plays have been translated in over ten languages and continue to be performed all over the world.

During these first years, while writing her plays, she kept making notes, in a big book, notes that would later become what she is now most famous for, her first novel: *The Notebook*.

This book, this collection, serves a dual purpose.

It gives an insight into a writer learning a new language, fighting with that new language, coming to terms with it, mastering and reinventing it for her on purpose.

It also shows the themes we are familiar with from her prose at an earlier stage, maturing, growing in complexity while being distilled towards their core meaning.

Translated for the first time in English, you will find here the nine plays she wrote in the time before her Trilogy: *The Notebook*, *The Proof* and *The Third Lie*.

Bart Smet, 2018

Ágota Kristóf received the European prize for French literature for *The Notebook* (1986), the Gottfried Keller Award in Switzerland (2001) and the Austrian Prize for European Literature (2008). She passed away at the age of seventy-five, in 2011, in Neuchâtel, where she lived the whole of the second part of her life.

JOHN AND JOE

Characters

JOHN

JOE

WAITER

SCENE ONE

A small square, terrace of a bar with two tables, chairs. In the back, the door to the bar.

JOHN enters from left, JOE from right. They are poorly dressed, but with a studied elegance. They are between 40 and 50 years old. They meet in the middle of the stage, before the tables.

JOHN: Hello, Joe!

JOE: Hello, John!

JOHN: What are you doing here?

JOE: Me?

JOHN: Yes, you.

JOE: I'm walking around. And you?

JOHN: Well, me too.

JOE: Oh!

JOHN: We could walk together.

JOE: We could …

JOHN: Or else, we could also sit down.

JOE: We could do that as well …

JOHN: Are you not thirsty?

JOE: Me?

JOHN: Yes, you.

JOE: No, not particularly.

JOHN: You surprise me! Me, I'm thirsty.

JOE: Ah!

JOHN: Would you like to keep me company?

JOE: If you like, John.

> *They sit down at a table. The WAITER arrives immediately. He stands stiff, with a little book and a pencil in his hands.*

JOHN: What are you having, Joe?

JOE: Me?

JOHN: Yes, you.

JOE: And you?

JOHN: The same as you.

JOE: *(To the waiter.)* A glass of water, please.

JOHN: *(Who didn't hear that.)* Two.

WAITER: *(Writing down.)* Two glasses of water. *(He returns to the bar.)*

JOHN: Nice day today, Joe.

JOE: Oh yes, John.

 (Silence.)

JOHN: And, how's things?

JOE: What?

JOHN: Everything.

JOE: Good.

JOHN: Oh, yes?

JOE: Yes.

JOHN: You surprise me.

JOE: Me?

JOHN: Yes, you. Listen Joe, you're getting on my nerves!

JOE: Me?

JOHN: Yes, you.

JOE: I'm getting on your nerves?

JOHN: Yes, you're getting on my nerves!

JOE: Why?

JOHN: When I ask you a question, you always say: me?

JOE: Me?

JOHN: You see?

JOE: What?

 (The WAITER returns, puts two glasses of water on the table and goes.)

JOHN: *(Looking at his glass.)* What's this Joe?

JOE: It's water, John.

JOHN: You ordered water, Joe?

JOE: Yes, John.

JOHN: Why, Joe?

JOE: Shouldn't I have, John?

JOHN: Waiter! Two coffees! You can be so irritating, Joe!

JOE: Me?

(JOHN doesn't reply, drums with his fingers on the table. The WAITER returns with two coffees and goes. JOE puts his two sugars in his coffee. JOHN doesn't.)

JOE: John?

JOHN: What is it?

JOE: You don't take sugar?

JOHN: No.

JOE: So, I can take it, your sugar?

JOHN: Why? You don't have any?

JOE: Me? I do.

JOHN: So, why do you want my sugar?

JOE: But, since you don't want any, John.

JOHN: Well, take it.

(JOE takes it and puts the two other pieces of sugar in his coffee. He stirs for a long time. He tries it. JOHN tries his too.)

JOHN: Is it good?

JOE: What?

JOHN: Your coffee.

JOE: Mine?

JOHN: Yes, yours. Is it good?

JOE: No, why?

JOHN: What do you mean, why?

JOE: Why do you ask me if it's good?

JOHN: Because.

JOE: And yours, John?

JOHN: What, mine?

JOE: Your coffee, is it good?

JOHN: Well, no.

JOE: Why?

JOHN: It needs sugar.

JOE: Mine's too sweet.

Overwhelming silence.

JOHN: I've got an idea, Joe!

JOE: You?

JOHN: Yes, me.

JOE: What?

JOHN takes one of the glasses and pours the water out onto the floor. He pours the two coffees in the glass and mixes them. Then he pours the coffees in the two cups and gives one to JOE.

JOHN: Try!

JOE: What?

JOHN: Your coffee.

JOE: I already tried it.

JOHN: Try again!

JOE tries it.

JOHN: And?

JOE: And what?

JOHN: Is it good?

JOE: No.

JOHN: But it's not too sweet now?

JOE: No, not really.

JOHN: So, what is it?

JOE: Nothing.

JOHN: But, why is it not good?

JOE: I don't know.

JOHN, in turn, tries his coffee.

JOE: Does it need more sugar?

JOHN: No.

JOE: So, is it good?

JOHN: No.

They look at each other, sadly.

JOHN: Joe, I have an idea.

JOE: You?

JOHN: Yes, me.

JOE: Again?

JOHN: Yes.

JOE: What?

JOHN: You'll see. Waiter!

The WAITER arrives.

JOHN: Two plum brandies, please.

WAITER: Two plums. *(He goes.)*

JOHN: What do you think of that?

JOE: Me?

JOHN: You.

JOE: Of what?

JOHN: Of my idea?

JOE: What idea?

JOHN: The brandies.

JOE: Ah!

JOHN: What, ah? You like a brandy, don't you?

JOE: A lot, John. Enormously.

JOHN: So, don't you think it was a good idea to order one?

JOE: Two, John. Two brandies.

JOHN: Well, naturally. Each his own. We could have started
with that. Why did you order water, Joe?

JOE: And why did you order coffee, John?

JOHN: You'll see, with these brandies, our coffees will taste much better.

The WAITER brings the brandies, and goes.

JOHN: Are you going to pour it in your coffee?

JOE: Me?

JOHN: You.

JOE: What?

JOHN: The brandy.

JOE: Oh no, John.

JOHN: Why?

JOE: I don't want to ruin my brandy.

JOHN: Well, me neither.

They drink their brandies.

JOE: That's good.

JOHN: That's good.

Silence.

JOE: Do you know Sauser?

JOHN: Sauser?

JOE: Sauser.

JOHN: Which Sauser?

JOE: Sauser.

JOHN: *(Thinks.)* Sauser?... Sauser?...

JOE: Who?

JOHN: Sauser.

JOE: I don't know him.

JOHN: You don't know him?

JOE: Me? No.

JOHN: Then, why do you ask me if I know him?

JOE: You don't know him either?

JOHN: No. And what about him, this Sauser?

JOE: What Sauser?

JOHN: Your Sauser!

JOE: My Sauser? It's not my Sauser.

JOHN: The Sauser you are talking about, then! What about him?

JOE: Nothing.

JOHN: Joe, you are completely mad. You talk to me about a Sauser that nobody knows! You're getting on my nerves. It's terrible how you get on my nerves!

JOE: Me?

JOHN: Yes!

JOE: Why?

JOHN: That's enough!

Silence.

JOE: Listen, John. I was talking like that, just to make conversation. There's nothing wrong with that.

JOHN: Never mind. Waiter!

JOE: Why are you calling him?

JOHN: We're having another brandy.

JOE: One?

JOHN: Two, if you want one as well, Joe. You'd like another brandy, don't you, Joe?

JOE: I wouldn't mind, John. I wouldn't mind.

The WAITER arrives.

JOHN: Two plum brandies. And get rid of these coffees. They're disgusting.

WAITER: Two plums. And two disgusting coffees to get rid of. *(He goes with the coffees.)*

Silence.

JOE: And his wife, you don't know her either?

JOHN: Whose wife?

JOE: Sauser's wife.

JOHN: What Sauser? Oh, no! Because you, you know her?

JOE: Who?

JOHN: His wife! And don't ask me whose wife!

JOE: Why?

JOHN: Do you know, yes or no, Sauser's wife?

JOE: No, I don't know her.

JOHN: Well then!

JOE: What then?

> *JOHN doesn't answer. The WAITER returns with two brandies and goes.*

JOE: I wonder, John …

JOHN: Yes, Joe?

JOE: I've thought about it quite a bit, John.

JOHN: About what, Joe?

JOE: Oh, it's not important.

JOHN: Just, tell me anyway, Joe.

JOE: I wouldn't like to annoy you, John.

JOHN: No, really, Joe?

JOE: Really not, John.

JOHN: Then, tell me, and immediately: what do you think about quite a bit, Joe?

JOE: But you are not going to get irritated, John? As with Sauser?

JOHN: What Sauser? Oh, no, Joe! You're unbearable!

JOE: Me?

JOHN: I'm going to scream!

JOE: Why, John?

JOHN: *(Sweet.)* Joe, my dear, very dear friend. Tell me, please, what do you think about quite a bit?

JOE: Me?

JOHN: Yes, you, my dear friend.

JOE: I don't know anymore, John. I forgot it. You made me so scared when you wanted to scream.

JOHN: But I just said that, like that, for a laugh.

JOE: Ah, OK.

JOHN: So, are you going to tell me, what you were thinking about?

JOE: I already told you that I didn't know anymore.

JOHN: Never mind. We'll pay.

JOE: Oh, yes, I know now.

JOHN: Oh, yes?

JOE: Yes, I was wondering how come that there are people who have money. A lot of money. All the time. They spend it and they still have some. Always. Do you understand any of that?

JOHN: But, Joe, there's nothing to understand. They have it, that's it.

JOE: And others, why don't they have any?

JOHN: That's very simple. They don't have any and that's that.

JOE: But those that do have it, from where does it get to them? That money must come from somewhere, no?

JOHN: Of course. They probably inherited it from their father.

JOE: And to their fathers, from where did that money come, to their fathers?

JOHN: Well, from their father.

JOE: But before there was a father that had money, to that first rich father, from where did it get to him?

JOHN: I don't know. He must have worked a lot.

JOE: You're not thinking it through, John. I know people that work all day. You can't work more than all day, can you? And they have no money, they have very little money. Just enough to eat, that's it.

JOHN: Thankfully, you don't mention yourself as an example.

JOE: Even so. Me too, I used to work, John.

JOHN: Ah, yes? When?

JOE: From time to time. Yes. When I was young.

JOHN: And you didn't earn a lot of money, Joe?

JOE: Oh no, John. You know all too well that it is not by working that you earn a lot of money.

JOHN: By doing what, then?

JOE: It's just that what I am wondering about.

JOHN: By being clever, maybe?

JOE: *(Very sad.)* Oh, John! You don't want to tell me that all those that have no money, also lack intelligence? Me, for example, or ... you?

JOHN: Of course, of course. You're absolutely right, Joe. I know a lot of intelligent people that have no money.

JOE: So?

JOHN: So what?

JOE: So, you see. It's also not a question of intelligence.

JOHN: Well, no.

JOE: But what then?

JOHN: I don't know anything about these things. A question of luck, or commercial sense. What do you want me to do about it? We haven't got any money, full stop. That's it. And we never will.

JOE: Exactly, John.

JOHN: Exactly, what?

JOE: Exactly, yes. How are we going to pay the bill?

JOHN collects the tickets on the table. He counts.

JOHN: Two glasses of water ... one franc, two coffee ... two francs, two plum brandies ... three francs, another two brandies...three francs. That makes nine francs, plus tip ... ten francs fifty, eleven francs ... divided between the two of us, five francs fifty each.

JOE: I apologise, John ...

JOHN: What are you apologising for, Joe?

JOE: I want you to take note that I only ordered one glass of water.

JOHN: What do you mean?

JOE: I'm mean to say, John, that I don't have any money on me. I have absolutely nothing on me.

JOHN: You don't seriously believe that I am going to buy you a coffee and two brandies.

JOE: I don't know, John. I'm not believing anything. The only thing I know is that I have absolutely nothing in my pockets.

JOHN: You shouldn't have sat down with me, then.

JOE: I believed, John …I thought that, maybe, you invited me for a drink.

JOHN: How can you have thought that, Joe? You know me. You know all too well that I do not have the means to invite someone for a drink.

JOE: That's why I ordered water, John. In case I was mistaken when it came to your invitation.

JOHN: But then afterwards, you did drink those two brandies, didn't you?

JOE: But not the coffee, John. I didn't drink the coffee. If at least you hadn't ordered those two disgusting coffees, John. That would have been two francs less.

JOHN: And your two glasses of water that would have been a franc less.

JOE: I didn't think they would makes us pay for those glasses of water, John. But those two coffees …

JOHN: Stop blaming me for those two coffees, Joe. After all it's not you paying for them.

JOE: Oh, no, John. I can't pay for them.

JOHN: But neither can I! I haven't got enough for the two of us. And even if I had enough, I wouldn't feel at all like offering you two brandies and a coffee.

JOE: I didn't drink the coffee, John. And you didn't have to …

JOHN: That's enough! What are we going to do?

JOE: We could have another two brandies.

JOHN: Are you mad? We already can't pay for the ones we had.

JOE: Exactly. What difference does it make if we can't pay for four or six brandies?

JOHN: No, no, I don't feel like it anymore. We have to do something.

JOE: We can only do one thing, John.

JOHN: What, Joe?

JOE: What we usually do when we don't have enough money to pay.

JOHN: You're right Joe. It's the only solution. But we could never again come back for a drink.

JOE: We won't come back.

JOHN: But then, we're good here.

JOE: We'll find another cafe, John. An even better one.

JOHN: Alright, let's go.

JOE: We should have another two brandies, John, before we go, if we never come back again, John.

JOHN: No, Joe, let's not exaggerate. Let's go.

They stand up and, on the tips of their toes, move away from the table towards the left exit. The WAITER arrives.

WAITER: Gentlemen!

JOHN and JOE stop, turn around and ashamed return to the table. The WAITER takes the hat JOE forgot on a chair.

WAITER: You forgot your hat, sir.

JOE: Oh, thank you!

JOHN: We didn't want to go yet … Heh, heh … We just wanted to stretch our legs a bit.

WAITER: Would you like something else?

JOHN: Well, no ... I don't think so. Joe, would you like to have something else?

JOE: Me?

JOHN: You.

JOE: Of course. A brandy.

JOHN: Nothing at all. You know very well that we're in a hurry.

JOE: We're in a hurry? To do what, John?

JOHN: To do a lot of things, Joe.

WAITER: We can settle the bill, then.

JOHN: Certainly, certainly. *(To JOE.)* Give me your wallet!

JOE: But, John, there's no ...

JOHN: Give it to me, I said!

JOE: *(While passing his wallet.)* The two francs that are in there, John, they're for my coffee tomorrow morning, and for my newspaper. You're not going to take them away from me, are you, John?

JOHN: I'm going to have to, Joe. *(He empties the wallet on the table.)* It's exact. Two francs and a ticket. A ticket for what, Joe?

JOE: It's a lottery ticket, John.

JOHN: *(To the WAITER.)* How much is it?

WAITER: That's nine francs, sir. Without the tip, sir.

JOHN, painstakingly, counts out ten francs fifty on the table. The WAITER takes the money and goes with the glasses.

JOE: Did you take my two francs, John?

JOHN: Of course, Joe, and your lottery ticket too. *(He returns the empty wallet to JOE.)* Your two francs and the ticket made for five francs, and you still owe me twenty-five cents, Joe.

JOE: I'll give them back to you tomorrow, John, your twenty-five cents.

JOHN: I trust you, Joe. Let's get out of here. But, what an idea to buy a lottery ticket, Joe!

SCENE TWO

One day later.

Same set.

JOHN enters from left, JOE from right. JOHN is dressed in new clothes, he is very cheerful. JOE is as before.

JOHN: Hello, Joe!

JOE: Hello, John!

JOHN: What are you doing here?

JOE: Me?

JOHN: Yes, you.

JOE: Walking around. And you?

JOHN: Me too.

JOE: Oh!

JOHN: We could walk together.

JOE: We could …

 Silence.

JOHN: You don't notice anything, Joe?

JOE: Me?

JOHN: You.

JOE: If I notice anything?

JOHN: Yes. You don't notice anything?

JOE: No, John. Nothing.

JOHN: Take a good look, Joe!

JOE: At what, John?

JOHN: My jacket, for example, or my tie, Joe.

JOE: I'm looking at them, John. *(He looks.)*

JOHN: Well then, Joe?

JOE: What then?

JOHN: You don't notice anything?

JOE: No nothing, John.

JOHN: You don't see they're new?

JOE: Oh! They're new?

JOHN: Doesn't it show?

JOE: Yes, now that you tell me, it clearly shows.

JOHN: What do you think of it, Joe?

JOE: Me?

JOHN: You.

JOE: Of what, John?

JOHN: Of my jacket and my tie?

JOE: They're nice, John. And they suit you very well.

Silence.

JOHN: How about we have a drink on the terrace?

JOE: I'd love to, John, but I only have ...

JOHN: Yes, I know. You only have two francs for your coffee tomorrow morning.

JOE: And for my newspaper, John.

JOHN: And for your newspaper. But today, I'm inviting you, Joe.

JOE: I'm sorry?

JOHN: I said, I'm inviting you. I'm buying you a drink.

JOE: You are buying me a drink?

JOHN: Yes, that's it.

JOE: Me?

JOHN: Yes, of course. Come!

JOE: Are you serious, John?

JOHN: Completely serious.

JOE: You're not joking?

JOHN: Not at all, Joe.

JOE: And you won't take my two francs, like yesterday, John?

JOHN: No, no, Joe, be calm. I'll pay for everything.

JOE: About those twenty-five cent, John, …

JOHN: Oh, forget about it.

JOE: I'm sorry, John, that I can't give them back to you now.

JOHN: I told you to forget about it.

JOE: You don't want them?

JOHN: No, Joe. I don't need them. I give them to you as a gift.

JOE: Thank you, John. Thank you very much.

JOHN: Come and sit down.

They approach the table. JOE hesitates.

JOE: Are you sure, John?

JOHN: *(Sits down.)* Will you come here!

JOE: Okay, okay. *(He sits down.)*

JOHN: What do you want to drink, Joe?

JOE: And you, John?

JOHN: A brandy. But you, you can have anything you feel like, Joe.

JOE: Really, John?

JOHN: You don't happen to be hungry, are you, Joe?

JOE: Me?

JOHN: Yes, you.

JOE: Why do you ask me that, John?

JOHN: Because you could eat something. A sandwich or whatever they have, really.

JOE: And you would even pay for that, John?

JOHN: Of course. I told you already.

JOE: And you, John, aren't you hungry?

JOHN: No, I had an enormous lunch. Snails, fish, steaks, cheese …

JOE: You ate all that, John?

JOHN: Yes. That's why I'm not eating now. I'll just be having a couple of brandies.

JOE: Several, John? Several brandies?

JOHN: As many as I feel like.

The WAITER arrives. He holds himself still with his notepad.

JOHN: That will be one plum brandy for me. Well, Joe, have you made up your mind?

JOE: Me?

JOHN: *(To the WAITER.)* Do you have sandwiches or something else to eat?

WAITER: Yes, sir. We have a ham sandwich and a sandwich with salami.

JOHN: Well, Joe? What do you like best? Ham or salami?

JOE: Ham or salami? I ... don't know, John. I really like ham and ... salami as well. Yes, I really like salami, and ... ham as well.

JOHN: Very well, Joe. *(To the WAITER.)* Bring us a ham sandwich and another with salami. *(To JOE.)* What do you want to drink? Wine or a beer, with your sandwiches?

JOE: Oh, John, I really like red wine, but I think I'd rather have ... I'd rather have a brandy.

JOHN: You can have a brandy after, Joe. *(To the WAITER.)* So, a half of red wine with the sandwiches, please.

(The WAITER notes it down and goes.)

JOE: Are you really going to pay for all that, John?

JOHN: Really, Joe, don't worry about it.

JOE: Do you really have enough money for all that, John? That is going to be terribly expensive.

(JOHN takes out his wallet. He pulls out a bundle of notes and shows them to JOE.)

JOHN: Look, Joe! One, two, three, four, five. Five hundred francs. And I still have some change on top of that.

JOE: Oh, John!

JOHN: So, you're at ease now, Joe?

JOE: Yes, John. I am completely at ease.

The WAITER brings the order, places it on the table and goes.

JOE: *(Looking at the sandwiches.)* And after all that, I can have a brandy as well, John? You did say I could have a brandy after, John?

JOHN: Yes, yes. Now eat!

JOE: *(Trying his ham sandwich.)* This is very good. There are even gherkins. *(He tries the other sandwich.)* This is also very good. They've put some mustard. I love mustard. A mustard without a sandwich is not a ham. *(He drinks some wine.)* This is also very good, this wine.

He eats with great relish, biting in one, then the other sandwich.

JOHN: I'm very happy to please you, Joe.

JOE: You are kind, John. You are very kind.

Silence. JOE chews.

JOHN: You're not very curious, Joe.

JOE: Me?

JOHN: Yes, you.

JOE: Why?

JOHN: You don't even ask me how I happen to have so much money?

JOE: It's true, John. It's true. I'm not very curious.

JOHN: It doesn't interest you to know why I have so much money?

JOE: Not really, John. The moment you have that money, I'm very happy for you.

JOHN: You wouldn't like me to tell you where that money came from?

JOE: Tell me, John, if you feel like telling me. But if you don't feel like it, don't tell me, John.

JOHN: Well, I'd like to tell you. That money, Joe, I won it in the lottery.

JOE: In the lottery?

JOHN: Yes, I've won a thousand francs in the lottery, Joe. But I've already spend nearly half. I have just five hundred francs and some change left.

JOE: You won a thousand francs, John? That's a lot of money. I am very happy for you, John.

JOHN: But I've already spend half.

JOE: You've done well, John.

JOHN: I've bought this jacket, shirts, ties ...

JOE: It's very nice, your jacket, John, and the tie also, and the shirt also. You've done well buying them.

Silence. JOE eats and drinks.

JOHN: You don't remember, Joe that I took a lottery ticket from you, yesterday?

JOE: Yes, I remember that. And my two francs also, you took those, John.

JOHN: *(Slowly.)* You see, Joe. That money that I won in the lottery, I won it with your ticket.

JOE: *(Stops chewing.)* With my ticket, John?

JOHN: Yes, with the ticket that I took from you yesterday, Joe. The draw was yesterday evening, and this morning I cashed in the thousand francs. Unfortunately, it was only a half ticket, Joe. If you would have bought a full ticket, I would have won two thousand francs. What an idea to buy a half ticket, Joe!

JOE: I'm sorry, John, I didn't have enough money to buy a full ticket.

JOHN: It's a shame, Joe. A real shame.

Silence. JOE has pushed his plate away with the leftovers of the sandwiches.

JOHN: You're not eating anymore, Joe?

JOE: Me?

JOHN: Yes, you.

JOE: No, John. I'm not eating anymore.

JOHN: Why, Joe?

JOE: I'm thinking, John.

Silence.

JOHN: What are you thinking about, Joe?

JOE: About my lottery ticket, John.

JOHN: And what do you think about it, Joe?

JOE: That you shouldn't have taken it from me, John.

JOHN: Why, Joe? You had to pay your part, no?

JOE: Yes. That's true, John. But my part, I should have been able to pay you back today, with what I would have won with my ticket.

JOHN: But Joe! Yesterday, we didn't know yet that your ticket was going to win a thousand francs! If it hadn't won, I would have lost three francs in this situation. I took a risk by taking your ticket, Joe. As much a risk as you, buying the ticket.

JOE: Yes, John. That's true. But, it is all too complicated for me.

JOHN: Finish your sandwiches, Joe.

JOE: I don't feel like it anymore, John.

JOHN: And the brandy, you still want that?

JOE: Yes, John. I'd love a brandy.

JOHN: Waiter! *(To JOE.)* You see, I am very nice, buying you so many things. I could have easily bought nothing. But I like you, Joe.

JOE: Me too, I like you, John.

The WAITER arrives.

JOHN: Two plum brandies.

WAITER: Two plums. *(He goes.)*

JOE: John?

JOHN: What is it, Joe?

JOE: You must not get angry, John, but I was thinking …

JOHN: What Joe?

JOE: I was thinking, if you were a real friend, you would share those thousand francs with me.

JOHN: Why, Joe?

JOE: Because .... that ticket ... was after all mine, John. You shouldn't have taken it from me.

The WAITER returns, places two brandies on the table and goes.

JOHN: Come on, Joe. I already explained to you that ticket wasn't yours anymore when it won a thousand francs. If only you had bought a full ticket, Joe.

JOE: I still think you should share, John. Or at least give me a small share.

JOHN: I have given you all this! This is it, your small share.

JOE: No, a little more, John. A bit more than that. You're not a real friend.

JOHN: You are making me sad, Joe. Put yourself in my place. If you had five hundred francs in your wallet, how much would you give me?

JOE: I don't know, John. I can't put myself in your place.

JOHN: Why not, Joe?

JOE: Because I have an old jacket, John, and because I have nothing in my wallet. I don't even have a wallet. I only have two francs for my coffee and my newspaper. So, I can't answer your question.

JOHN: But imagine what it feels like to have a new jacket and five hundred francs in your wallet. Try to imagine, Joe.

JOE: I can't do that, John, without a new jacket and without a wallet.

Silence.

JOE: I have an idea.

JOHN: You?

JOE: Yes, me.

JOHN: You surprise me! What idea, Joe?

JOE: If you would give me, just for a moment, your jacket with the wallet, maybe I could put myself in your place, John.

JOHN: Eh?

JOE: Yes, and maybe, I could understand you, John. And I wouldn't tell you again that you're not a real friend, John.

JOHN: Sure you wouldn't tell me again, Joe?

JOE: Sure, John. You don't want to try, John?

JOHN: Well ... Why not? We can try. *(He takes his jacket off.)* But only for a very short moment, Joe.

JOE: That's it, John.

They exchange their jackets.

JOHN: Well then, Joe?

JOE: You couldn't pass me your tie as well, could you, John? I really like it. With that tie, I'll come even closer to putting myself in your place.

JOHN gives his tie. JOE puts it on.

JOHN: Well then, Joe?

JOE: Wait a bit.

Silence. JOE closes his eyes. He is happy.

JOHN: Well then, Joe?

JOE: What?

JOHN: Can you put yourself in my place, Joe?

JOE: Very well, John.

JOHN: So, what do you think?

JOE: Nothing, John. How much is there left in your wallet, John?

JOHN: *(Counts.)* Four francs sixty, Joe.

JOE: You can keep that, John. Anyway, I owe you three francs twenty-five cent, from yesterday. The rest I give you. And I also give you those two brandies. And as for your dinner, John, I'll give you that as well, because I can't really go about that differently. But you shouldn't have eaten so much, John. It's not healthy to eat so much.

JOHN: I don't understand, Joe.

JOE: That's a shame, John. I'll explain it to you some other time. I'm in a hurry. Waiter, I'd like to pay! I'd better go and buy some shirts.

JOHN: You would like to pay, Joe?

JOE: Yes, I would like to pay.

JOHN: With what, Joe?

JOE: With this, John. *(He taps on the wallet.)* This jacket, John, it's not really to my taste, but, oh well.

JOHN: Give it back to me, now.

JOE: What, John?

JOHN: My jacket, Joe!

JOE: Maybe I'll give it back, when I've bought another one, John.

JOHN: And my wallet!

JOE: *(Sad.)* That was *my* ticket, John. You've taken too much advantage of it. I even leave you the shirts.

JOHN stands up, grabs JOE by the jacket.

JOHN: Give me back my jacket and my money!

They tug each other without hitting one another. They turn the table over.

JOE: You are going too far, John. Now I'm going to have to pay for the broken glasses.

JOHN: Give me my jacket! My tie! My wallet!

The WAITER arrives, separates them.

WAITER: What's going on?

JOE: He wants to take my money.

JOHN: He has taken my jacket, my tie, my wallet!

JOE straitens his jacket, his tie.

JOE: I want to file a complaint. He attacked me. Tried to take my wallet.

JOHN: He's lying! It's mine! Everything is mine! The tie, the jacket, the wallet.

JOE: That's ridiculous. How could I have taken his jacket and his tie?

WAITER: It's true. How could he – how could I have – ?

JOHN: *(To the WAITER.)* Even so, you saw for yourself: before, it was me who had them.

WAITER: Aye, me! If I looked at the jacket and tie of all those that I serve …

JOHN: I gave him the jacket with the wallet, for a short moment.

WAITER: No kidding! And the tie?

JOHN: The tie as well. I lent it to him for a short time. Besides, you can see that the jacket is too big for him.

JOE: Not at all. I like it loose fitting. I like to feel comfortable.

JOHN: Everything is mine!

WAITER: There is an officer at the corner of the street. You sort it out with him.

JOE: I'll settle the bill first. How much do I owe you?

WAITER: With the broken glasses and the cracked plate, you owe me twenty-two francs, sir.

JOE gives a one hundred franc note.

JOE: Make it thirty francs.

JOHN: You are mad!

WAITER: Thank you, sir. Thank you very much, sir. You are a true gentleman. One can see that.

JOHN: Oh, yes! And he's a true friend.

JOE: We can go and find that officer now.

The WAITER takes JOHN by the arm and they all exit.

SCENE THREE

Same décor. JOE enters from left, JOHN from right. JOE is very well dressed. He has over his arm the jacket he took from JOHN in Scene 2.

JOHN: Hello, Joe!

JOE: Hello, John!

JOHN: What are you doing here?

JOE: I'm walking around. And you?

JOHN: Well, I got out of prison, Joe.

JOE: Oh! How did that go, John?

JOHN: As usual, Joe.

JOE: It wasn't too hard?

JOHN: Not too much so. I slept all the time.

JOE: What did you get for breakfast, John?

JOHN: Lentil soup, Joe.

JOE: With lard in it?

JOHN: Yes, Joe. With some lard in it.

JOE: That's not bad that, John.

JOHN: It was quite good, Joe.

JOE: And last evening, what did they give you to eat?

JOHN: Potato soup, Joe.

JOE: With a piece of sausage in it?

JOHN: Yes, with a little piece of sausage in it.

JOE: And with bread?

JOHN: Yes, with a nice chunk of bread, Joe.

JOE: That's not bad that, John.

JOHN: It was quite good, Joe.

   Silence.

JOHN: I'm thirsty. We could have a drink.

JOE: How much money have you got, John?

JOHN: I have the four francs sixty that were left in my wallet from yesterday. And you, Joe?

JOE: I still have about ten francs or so, John.

JOHN: And … the rest?

JOE: I've bought myself some trousers, John. And shirts.

JOHN: They're nice, your trousers, Joe. And your shirt, as well.

JOE: And I bought a hat.

JOHN: It's very nice, your hat, Joe.

JOE: And I also bought another jacket. I give you yours back, John. It didn't half please me.

JOHN: Oh, thank you, Joe! I like it very much. *(He puts the jacket on.)* And the tie, Joe?

JOE: It's in the pocket of the jacket, John.

JOHN finds the tie, puts it on.

JOHN: Thanks, Joe. That's very kind, Joe.

JOE: There was still two hundred francs left after my purchases, John.

JOHN: And what did you do with it, Joe?

JOE: I paid your bail, John.

JOHN: Ah! It was you?

JOE: Who else could it have been, John? Do you have any other friends aside from me, John?

JOHN: Well, no, Joe. I don't.

JOE: You see? Me neither, John. I don't have any other friends. That's why I got you out of prison. And I have withdrawn my complaint, John.

JOHN: Thank you. Thank you very much, Joe.

JOE: But you will be tried for public disturbance, John. I couldn't do anything to stop that. But I paid your bail, John.

JOHN: Thank you, Joe. Well, shall we have a drink?

JOE: Yes. And each pays for his.

JOHN: As usual.

JOE: As usual.

They sit down at their table. The WAITER arrives.

JOHN: A plum brandy.

JOE: A plum brandy.

WAITER: Two plums. *(He goes.)*

JOE: *(Counting his money.)* After having paid for my brandy, I'll keep two francs for my coffee ...

JOHN: And your newspaper, Joe.

JOE: And for my newspaper. That will leave me enough to buy a lottery ticket.

JOHN: Let's hope you win, Joe!

JOE: I'll buy you a lot of things, if I win, John.

JOHN: Thank you, Joe. Thank you very much.

The WAITER arrives and puts the brandies down. He goes. JOHN and JOE drink their brandies.)

JOE: That's good.

JOHN: That's good.

Silence.

JOHN: It's a nice day, Joe.

JOE: Oh yes, John.

JOHN: I'm going to buy myself another brandy, Joe.

JOE: Yes, John?

JOHN: Yes. I missed that a lot in prison, brandies. You know, Joe.

JOE: I know, John. It's what's missing the most in prison.

JOHN: Waiter! A plum brandy!

JOE: Two!

JOHN: You're having one as well, Joe?

JOE: I will only buy a half ticket, John.

JOHN: You're right, Joe.

(The WAITER brings the two brandies and goes.)

JOE: Having thought about it, I'm not buying a ticket at all.

JOHN: No, Joe?

JOE: No. I am going to buy me another brandy, and you as well, John. I'll buy you one. It's the least I could do for a friend who has just come out of prison.

JOHN: Thank you, Joe. You are kind, Joe.

JOE: Why would I buy a ticket, John? I have all I want. Shirts, ties, even a new hat.

JOHN: Well, yes, and me too, I have all I want, Joe.

They drink their brandy.

JOE: Do you know … *(He thinks.)* Huguenin?

JOHN: Huguenin?

JOE: Yes, Huguenin.

JOHN: Which Huguenin?

End of play.

Neuchatel, 1972

THE LIFT KEY

Characters

THE WOMAN

THE HUSBAND

THE DOCTOR

THE GAME KEEPER

A round room.

A round table.

A gothic window.

Before the curtain goes up, there is a long howl.

Medieval music, a melancholy ballad.

The curtain is raised.

A WOMAN sits by the window, in a wheelchair, her back turned to the audience. Her long blond hair swirls over the back of the chair.

In a sweet and softly singing voice, she says.

THE WOMAN: There was once a young and beautiful chatelaine. On the borders of a mountainous land, in her castle, perched on the top of a high rock, she dreamed, she waited.

One winter's day, when a snow storm raged, a stranger knocked at the door of the castle. It was a young man, handsome. When she saw him, the chatelaine knew he was the one she was waiting for. He called himself a prince, driven out of his country by the jealousy of treacherous lords. He asked for hospitality.

He lived in the castle until spring. Then he left again, promising to return when he had won his power and his people back.

By the window, the chatelaine followed him with her eyes, with her eyes full of tears, waving her embroidered handkerchief long after the black silhouette of the prince had disappeared in the mists over the plane. *(Pause.)*

The plain was soon covered by an intense green, toned down in places with touches of yellow rape and the tender white of wild daisies.

It was summer. A mad, stormy summer that drove its lightning deep into the sad heart of the chatelaine.

Shooting stars fell on the sun bereft face of the nights. Into the sombre lakes, into the deep forests, the stars fell like tears.

The moon lit the still plain with a cruel indifference, while the landscape wrought with unspeakable suffering and a nameless anguish wandered through the trees.

The blue eyes of the chatelaine grew larger, became dark. Under her full white dress, drops of sweat fell from her cold shoulders onto her burning hips.

Then, came autumn.

The evil spirits washed their blood soaked-hands and mouths and flew south, north, over the current of the wind.

The plain became yellow, then brown. Endless soft rain beat down on the land. Rotten torn leafs clung onto the window.

The chatelaine looked at the plain.

She had found her confident smile again.

She thought of the burning kiss of the separation, she thought of the promises of her prince.

The first snow fell.

Winter had settled for eternity, it seemed.

The chatelaine embroidered, looking at the frost, the palm trees and the flowers – silvery souvenirs of the wind – engraved on the sombre panes of her window.

Sometimes, she leaned forward, blew on the glass pane, cleared a circle with her breath in the white pattern, peered over the plain until the image reformed.

The never-ending days dissolved one into the other, dissolved into nights, into the greyness of the sky, into the virgin white of the plain.

It was spring again.

The flowers, the birds, hope.

Then, summer.

And autumn again. Calm, soothing.

Another winter. Spring once more.

And the chatelaine at her window.

Full of hope, smiling, blonde and beautiful.

And, always, before the window, the plain.

A barren plain, wild, where nothing moved but the high grass, rippled by the southern wind that brought with it mysteries, passions, promises from another place.

Later, years later, the chatelaine had nightmares: a white horse, a mad horse, galloping unbridled through the immensity of the wild plain, stopping under the windows of the castle, neighing, howling at the moon, like dogs, like wolves.

(Pause.)

A black silhouette, standing out against the snow, his silhouette, bend, wavering ... The trail of blood, of his blood, on the snow ... a red trail, like the stars ... His collapse! His arms held out ... His lips ... His face wrought by suffering ... As in the pain of ... desire.

Years passed.

Nothing moved on the plain.

The grass waved, the colours changed.

One day the chatelaine turned away from her window.

A dense mist prevented her from looking at the plain.

She turned. She saw her room. A table. A bed.

What am I doing here? She asked herself. What am I doing in this solitude?

It had been a long time since she had gone down to the communal hall where her brother ruled as lord and master over the castle and over his numerous children.

It had been a long time since she had seen them.

A taciturn old servant maid brought her meals, her linen, made her bed.

It had been a long time since ... anything mattered to her but the plain.

A long time ...

How many winters had passed?

How many springs, summers, autumns?

She didn't know anymore.

On her lips still burned the impassioned and tender kiss ...

She approached a mirror.

An unknown woman looked at her.

An old woman.

She sat down at her small desk.

She wrote a letter.

She slept in her freshly made bed.

She closed her eyes.

A knight dressed in black galloped on his white mount from the borders of the plain towards her castle, growing, growing still

– No, I don't want to, I don't want to anymore, she cried, covering her eyes that she knew were encroached with wrinkles.

A young face bent over her dried lips and she was ashamed.

– It's too late, she said swallowing, and her prince covered her pitifully with his black cape.

Her brother read the letter.

She wanted to be buried somewhere on the plain.

The last wishes of a mad woman.

They buried her in the family tomb.

Of the prince, nobody has ever heard.

Short mad laugh. The music stops. The same voice, but more ordinary, continues.

I had more luck. My own prince returns every evening. I haven't waited in vain. He never left me. I don't know solitude. In the morning he goes off into the plain, but he returns every evening. For twenty years, he has been returning every evening. The rest of the time, it is true, I am alone. I wait for him. But what a beautiful thing the wait, when you are sure ... *(Wild, she turns to the audience.)* Of what? Sure of what then? *(Shaking her head.)* Sure ... of the return of ... the loved one. While I am waiting for him ... I look over the plain. I embroider as the chatelaines of another time, the sad chatelaines of times past ...

But I'm not unhappy!

I am happy! Happy! *(Mad cry.)* Hoo!

(Calm.) I am happy. Every evening he returns.

My prince! *(In an objective tone.)* It is not a prince.

He is an architect. *(Pause.)* Anyway, that's why he leaves every morning. To work. If he didn't work we couldn't pay for the bills of our castle.

Which he built for us. For me. *(Glum.)* A love nest.

(Dreamy.) Perched on the tip of a high rock. As in the stories. *(Dry.)* Far from the pollution of the city. Far from the plain.

Here, there's nothing but fir trees. Pure air. For me.

He, poor man, he has to go down each morning into the plain. For his office. For his work, Poor man. Poor man? Yes, poor man. First he has to take the lift. Then he has to take the car. He has thirty kilometres to go to reach his office. The poor man! The telephones ringing. People bothering him. Never a minute of peace.

While I ...

Well protected by walls ...

(Lively.) Nobody can get up here.

There is no path that leads here.

The only way to get here is a lift.

But you need a key.

Nobody has the key of the lift.

Except my husband.

(Pause.)

Me neither, I don't have the lift key.

(Pause.)

But then, I have no reason to take the lift.

The pure air of the forest enters here without me having to go and look for it. I just have to open the window.

(She opens the window. A big breath. The rustle of trees, the song of birds.)

It's wonderful!

(Pause.)

In the beginning, I had the lift key. I could go for a walk in the forest. I couldn't go as far as the city, obviously. That was too far, without a car. But I often walked in the forest. I liked walking in the forest.

I was thrilled to hear and see the birds, the squirrels, and even simply the leaves of the trees that moved in the wind, glistened in the sun light.

(Pause.)

It was in spring ... I was walking, marvelled by all these beautiful things of nature when, how horrible! A man appeared before me, under an oak, with a barrel gun over his shoulder. He was surely only a gamekeeper, but I was very afraid. Even more so because he had blonde hair, a beard and blue eyes, while my husband has black eyes and black hair and is clean shaven.

The man held out a bunch of flowers towards me.

THE GAMEKEEPER: *(A faraway voice that the WOMAN hears in her imagination.)* Here. They are the first flowers from our forest.

THE WOMAN: 'Our forest' felt a bit strong to me, because it associated us in a way ... let's say, intimate, as if we had something in common, him, me and this forest ...

Since I didn't move, he came closer to me and he looked me in the eyes, smiling.

Then I felt something terrible. It was certainly fear, agony, anyway, my heart beat violently and I wanted to scream but I didn't scream. I took the flowers, I simply said thank you, and fled. I threw myself in the lift with a sense of relief that was painful. When I arrived into my room, I threw the bouquet through the window.

(She closes the window.)

That evening, I told my husband everything. He smiled.

THE HUSBAND: *(Faraway voice, as above.)* It would be better if you didn't go out without me.

THE WOMAN: Gently he took the lift key from me.

THE HUSBAND: *(As above.)* It's for your own good. Something serious could happen to you. You could be attacked. A woman alone in such a big forest …

THE WOMAN: He kissed me.

(Pause.)

I didn't have the key anymore.

I couldn't leave my room anymore.

I looked through the window. I waited for the evening. I awaited his return.

But soon I started having problems with my legs.

It wasn't too bad. I had pins and needles in my legs.

As I sat down all day, that was normal. But it bothered me. It was very distressing to me. I told my husband about it. He kissed me.

THE HUSBAND: *(As above.)* You just have to walk in the room. Turn around the table.

THE WOMAN: He always knew what was the best thing to do.

(Pause.)

So I started walking around the table. Like this.

(She turns around the table in her wheelchair.)

And I closed the window, so spring wouldn't come in.

My urge to walk in the forest was so big.

But I couldn't anymore. I shouldn't walk in the forest anymore.

So, I walked around the table. *(She does.)*

Then I sat before my window, I took up my work, I embroidered, waiting for the evening.

(Pause.)

But I had more and more trouble with my legs.

I didn't want to get up anymore.

I had pins and needles in my legs.

I complained so much, my husband decided to consult a doctor, Claude. He was a college friend of his. A man to be trusted. My husband had invited him one evening. We talked together, the three of us, in earnest.

THE DOCTOR: *(Faraway voice, as above.)* It's nothing serious. A small intervention will sort everything.

THE WOMAN: My husband gave me a smile. Claude gave me an injection.

(Pause.)

When I woke up, I felt really good. The pins and needles had disappeared. But I couldn't move my legs anymore. I couldn't shift them anymore. *(As a terrible secret.)* I couldn't walk anymore.

(Pause.)

He had to kill the nerves.

My husband gave me a wheelchair as a present. I can still go around the table.

(She does.) I can still embroider ... A chatelaine who embroiders, while waiting for her prince...

(Suddenly she throws her embroidery, and with a mad voice.)

But I can never, never again, walk in the forest, and be afraid – but was it fear? – of a game keeper with blue eyes, and ... a bunch of flowers ... from our forest.

(Sobs, then, calmed down, she opens the window. The sound of trees, the wind, birds. A faraway song appears, a love song that sometimes changes into a whisper.)

I have an evil nature. I am never happy. Now that the trouble with my legs was gone, I started to suffer from other discomforts. My ears. I had ringing in my ears. My poor husband! In the evening, when he came back from a day of hard work, instead of finding a consoling, cheerful woman, he found nothing but moaning. My ears are ringing ... I can't stand the noise of birds ... I can't stand the silence ... I can't stand the noise of the city.

(Pause.)

Claude came back. His frank expression inspired confidence...

THE DOCTOR: *(Voice as before.)* It's nothing. A small intervention ...

(Pause.)

THE WOMAN: I don't hear the birds anymore. Or any other sound. I didn't even hear my husband's voice. *(She closes the window.)* But I very quickly learned how to read his lips.

THE HUSBAND: *(As above.)* If we want to protect our love ... This is nothing, my sweet. Think of our happiness. I am here. We love each other.

THE WOMAN: I embroider. It is winter. The lights of the city go up very early in the evening. Well before my husband returns.

The lights of the city!

Oh, how I wish to be there!

See people, hear voices!

Hear voices?

See people?

(Pause.)

The lift key ...

Thirty kilometres, without a car, through the forest, on foot ...

(Sniggering.) With which feet?

(Softly.) I have no more legs, no more ears, no more eyes.

(She turns to the audience.)

I don't have eyes, either. No. Claude came back. So the lights of the city wouldn't bother me anymore ... to preserve our love ... a small intervention ... painless, of course. *(Pause.)* He had to kill the nerves. He is a very capable surgeon. Reliable.

(Pause.)

Yes, I have my eyes. They are blue. But I can't see anymore.

I have legs but I can't walk anymore.

I have ears, but I don't hear anything. Nothing! Not even my own voice. My voice! My voice!

(A long howl.)

(Calmed down.) My husband thinks that I am more beautiful like this. He says that now my eyes always keep their soft and dreamy expression. While before it happened sometimes that he could detect in my look a sparkle of hostility or even hate.

What an idea!

(She calms down, turns back to the window, she opens it. She takes her blonde wig off, throws it. Dirty grey hairs pour over the back of the chair. From the window enter the faraway sounds of a big city, of a highway nearby, cars, trains, sirens of factories or ambulances, etc ...)

(With a broken aged voice.) So, what's the point? I have had a beautiful life. Calm, peaceful. With the man I loved. Luckily, I still have him. He hasn't abandoned me. He still comes back every night. He won't stop coming. My own prince. What would become of me without him?

(Pause.)

The gamekeeper too. He must have become older ... The birds are certainly not the same anymore. So many years have passed. How long does a bird live? Two years? Fifteen years? I have no idea. How long do people live? An eternity, it seems.

(Pause.)

It looks like the city is coming closer. My husband told me. I understand everything he says, following the movement of his lips with my fingers.

THE HUSBAND: *(As above.)* There is almost nothing left of the big plain.

Buildings, roads devour the land … It's terrible!

Luckily you can't hear anymore, because the noise of the city has come closer. Noise is very bad for your health, for the mental health of people. There are people that have become mad because of noise. You are lucky, you.

THE WOMAN: Yes, I am lucky. I don't hear anything anymore. It doesn't matter to me that the city is coming closer. The noises don't bother me anymore. Or the lights of the city. My husband, my prince will soon return. I wait for him. I love him.

(She turns brusquely. She is an old wrinkled woman, untidy, with mad eyes.)

(Ironic.) Besides, If I love him or not, what does that matter now? I only have him. So, I love him and I wait for him. What else could I do? There's no one else to love, here. Or to hate. There's only me. *(Wild.)* And I hate myself! Dirty old impotent woman, I hate you! There's nothing left for you to do then throw yourself out of the window, into the abyss, and break your deaf and blind face on the rocks!

(Pause.)

But why? Why suddenly all this hate?

What have I done? Nothing. That's it, isn't it. I haven't done anything! Nothing!

When the city arrives at the foot of our rock, I will throw myself down so people can cover me with their spit and insults and my face crashes on the stones of the street.

(Pause.)

I won't hear the insults anymore. Not one accusation, not one sarcastic remark can touch me. Nothing can touch me.

(She closes the window, the noise stops. She continues, softly.)

There's nothing to be done. I can't hear anymore. I don't even hear my voice anymore. I can't hear my own voice! *(Long howl.)*

(Two men enter. The HUSBAND and the DOCTOR. They stop close to the door. Another long howl.)

THE HUSBAND: It has been like that for months.

THE DOCTOR: Poor Jacques! It's very painful to listen to.

THE HUSBAND: Yes, because you'd say … you'd say she is suffering.

THE DOCTOR: What could she still be suffering from?

THE WOMAN: Darling? Are you there? *(She holds her arms out to her husband.)*

THE DOCTOR: It is mainly painful for you.

THE WOMAN: Are you there, my prince? Come, come closer.

THE HUSBAND: When she howls like that, it seems to me she isn't happy.

THE DOCTOR: Not happy? Never mind that now. She was never happy. We troubled ourselves enough with her. Right now, it is your inner calm that is at stake.

(The WOMAN 'listens', tilting forward like an animal.)

THE HUSBAND: My inner calm isn't important. I just can't hear her suffering like that.

THE DOCTOR: And at night, the same circus, I suppose. You don't look well at all, poor friend. How can you continue your work in such conditions?

THE WOMAN: Darling, I know you are there. Come, I waited so long for you.

(She moves up a bit with her chair towards her HUSBAND. The HUSBAND drops at his wife's feet, she strokes his hair, follows with her fingers the movement of his lips.)

You are tired, aren't you darling?

THE HUSBAND: Yes, a little. *(Whispering.)* Do something, Claude.

THE WOMAN: Is there someone else?

THE HUSBAND: It's Claude, my darling. *(He pulls the DOCTOR by the arm, so his wife can touch him.)* You see, it's Claude. Touch him. You recognise him, don't you?

THE WOMAN: Oh, Claude!

(The DOCTOR gets a needle ready. He takes the WOMAN's arm. The HUSBAND takes the WOMAN's face in both hands.)

THE DOCTOR: A small intervention ... Painless, that goes without saying.

THE HUSBAND: She won't cry anymore?

THE DOCTOR: No, she won't cry anymore.

THE WOMAN: *(Freeing her arm and face.)* Claude again? Why? What else can he take from me? My life, is that it? It is all that I have left.

THE DOCTOR: No, no, come on. You still have many, happy years before you, madam.

THE WOMAN: Darling! You shake your head. *(Pause.)* Oh, I know! I know what you want from me. My voice! That's it, isn't it? Yes, that's it! But I don't want to! No! Not my voice, you hear! My life, if you want, but not my voice! No!

(She grabs the DOCTOR's bag and takes a scalpel from it.)

THE DOCTOR: Watch out! Jacques! Watch out! The scalpel! She took it! Jacques ...!

(The WOMAN has thrust the scalpel in her HUSBAND's back. The HUSBAND collapses. The DOCTOR leans over the body. The WOMAN opens the window, through which enters the faraway sound of the city and a highway close by.)

Jacques! She killed you, that ... that horrible woman...

THE WOMAN: *(Softly.)* No, not my voice. Even if I can't hear it anymore, others could hear it. Someone else ... Many others ... *(Crescendo.)* I have to tell them ... I will tell them everything ... Listen to me!

End of play.

A PASSING RAT

Characters

BREDUMO-KEB

ROLL

RAT

BRIG-GEORGE

A JOURNALIST

A PHOTOGRAPHER

MM BREDUMO

ARGAS

MM ARGAS

NOEMI

The stage is divided in two, in such a way,
that while one part is visible, the other is not.

1. THE ROOM:

A bed, a night table, a few chairs.

A window in the back, a door to the left. Curtains at the window
and the door. A carpet. Paintings on the wall.

2. THE LIVING ROOM:

A coffee table, a bar, sofas, a French window in the back.

Between the two sets, a swing door.

SCENE ONE

Roll, Brig, Rat

The Living room. ROLL sits in a wheelchair, dressed as a judge. He wears the mask of an old man that represents BREDUMO. He takes the judge's mantle off and hangs it somewhere. He enters the room, stands up, takes the mask off and throws it on the wheelchair, which he rolls into a corner. ROLL is a young man, tall and handsome. Standing in the middle of the room, he recites a poem.

ROLL: It seems to me that the sky
    prepares itself for rain
    or maybe
    while I was crying
    it had already rained.

    Certainly
    above my palms
    the air had taken on colours
    and siding the dark clouds
    the blue is transparent.

    The sun is still there
    Graceless, about to fall
    The lights have dug in their roots
    all along the road.

    In the unsteady evening
    a free bird takes its sidelong flight
    the wind has reopened the wounds of the sky

    (Enter BRIGG, dressed as a prison guard. He carries a heavy board.)

BRIG: Look at that! The gentleman recites poetry. And me, I work, I slave away.

ROLL: I didn't ask you for anything.

BRIG: Silence! Besides, poetry is not allowed.

ROLL: There's nobody around.

BRIG: There's me.

ROLL: Alright, alright. I'm so bored.

BRIG: The gentleman is bored? Me, I work.

BRIGG places the board on the bed, grabs the table and the chairs and puts them away in the corner of the room. After having removed the curtains, he draws bars on the window. He also draws a rectangle with bars on the door. He rolls up the carpet, takes the paintings of the wall. He piles everything up in the same corner. ROLL follows his movements with much interest.

ROLL: Well, you'd say I am in prison.

BRIG: It looks like it.

ROLL: And why would I be in prison?

BRIG: We don't know yet. We're in the beginning of the play.

ROLL: Will we know later on?

BRIG: The gentleman asks too many questions. The gentleman is curious. Me, I do what they told me to do. You see me asking questions? You keep quiet.

BRIG leaves.

ROLL: My prison. It's so beautiful! And it's so cold! And so dark! It's fantastic!

BRIG returns with a can.

BRIG: Here's your can, young man.

ROLL: What's that for?

BRIG: It's to replace the toilets.

ROLL: *(Looking at it closely.)* But it's almost full already!

BRIG: Of course. It has to be authentic.

ROLL: It smells bad.

BRIG: Yes. It stinks. It's perfect.

BRIG leaves.

ROLL: It's authentic. Perfect. *(He sniffs.)* I would have preferred it without the can.

ROLL sits on the bed, looks at his room transformed into a prison. Then he stands up and recites with emphasis.

Do you know the evening whisper
of the damp walls
and the blinding light fixed

on shapeless faces ...

RAT emerges from underneath the wall. He wears a rat's mask.

RAT: I am a rat!

ROLL: Nice to meet you. My name is Roll.

RAT: I am going to bite you! Yes. Krrr. I am going to bite you!

ROLL backs away. RAT chases him. ROLL bangs on the door.

ROLL: Brig! Brig! Guard! There's a rat. I don't want any rats!

RAT takes his rat mask off.

RAT: But be quiet! I was joking around. It's only me.

ROLL: Ah, it's you, Rat-the-Bastard? What are you doing here?

RAT: Nothing. I just want to have a bit of fun.

ROLL: But how did you get into this room? I mean, in here, in prison?

RAT: On my belly. By lifting the set a bit. With this rat face, nobody pays attention to me. A passing rat, it's oh so common ...

ROLL: You're so clever! If Brig comes, you have to hide.

RAT: Brig? What is he playing?

ROLL: A prison guard. He puts a lot of effort in it. He has always been very conscientious.

RAT: Too much even. That guy, he makes me want to be sick.

ROLL: There's a can if you want to be sick.

RAT: Oh! A real one! It stinks!

ROLL: Watch the language!

RAT: Pfff. In a prison.

ROLL: This is a noble prison.

RAT: What do you know about that?

ROLL: Well, at least I hope it is.

RAT: You take yourself very seriously, today!

ROLL: Mind your own business. Besides, I am supposed to be alone here. Your presence is completely superfluous.

SCENE TWO

ROLL, RAT, THE JOURNALIST, THE PHOTOGRAPHER, BRIG

A knock on the door. RAT hides under the bed. The rectangle, drawn on the door by BRIG, opens. THE JOURNALIST sticks his head through the opening.

THE JOURNALIST: The press!

> *ROLL opens the door. The head of THE JOURNALIST remains in the rectangle. THE PHOTOGRAPHER enters.*

THE JOURNALIST: Help me, please!

ROLL: Don't damage the door. It's cardboard. It's not solid.

THE JOURNALIST: Neither is my head.

ROLL: You shouldn't just stick it anywhere.

THE PHOTOGRAPHER: It's your ears that hold you back. They're too big. You should clip them a bit.

THE JOURNALIST: My ears, never! They're the tools of my trade. *(He manages to free himself.)* Finally!

ROLL: You've damaged it!

THE JOURNALIST: *(Feeling his head.)* No, I'm okay.

ROLL: The door!

THE PHOTOGRAPHER: I'll fix that. *(He fixes the rip with tape.)*

ROLL: Gentlemen, take a seat.

> *ROLL sits down on the bed. THE JOURNALIST wants to take a chair.*

ROLL: Leave the chair. It's not here. It's in my room.

> *THE JOURNALIST sits down on the floor. THE PHOTOGRAPHER takes pictures. ROLL poses.*

ROLL: Which paper do you write for?

THE JOURNALIST: 'Cithemu'.

ROLL: What did you say?

THE JOURNALIST: Ci: Cinema, The: Theatre, Mu: Music. 'Cithemu. It's a biannual about cinema, theatre and music.

ROLL: Is it a big and famous biannual?

THE JOURNALIST: We have no idea yet. We are preparing the first number.

THE PHOTOGRAPHER: *(To ROLL.)* Could you be a bit more distressed?

ROLL: With pleasure. *(Poses.)* Is this okay?

THE PHOTOGRAPHER: Yes. But, don't squint.

ROLL: And are there many of you working for this paper?

THE JOURNALIST: The two of us. That's enough.

THE PHOTOGRAPHER: Now, take on a rebellious pose.

ROLL: Like this?

THE PHOTOGRAPHER: Perfect. But, don't squint.

ROLL: *(To THE JOURNALIST.)* What are you writing?

THE JOURNALIST: My article on you. You are the hero of the most stirring political trail of these last ten years.

ROLL: Oh! Really?

THE JOURNALIST: You didn't know?

ROLL: I did, of course, I did. But I was unaware that my trail had ... created such a stir.

THE JOURNALIST: Does that bother you?

ROLL: No, no, quite the opposite. I am very proud.

THE JOURNALIST: Who wouldn't be?

ROLL: But, what are you writing then? You haven't asked me anything yet.

THE JOURNALIST: I am describing the scene, the ambience, the atmosphere ...

ROLL: Don't forget the can.

THE JOURNALIST: The can? *(He looks into the can, sniffs.)* That's fantastic! You've done all that already?

ROLL: Eh ... Yes ... It's authentic.

THE JOURNALIST: A picture of the can! This is delicious!

THE PHOTOGRAPHER moves the can around a couple of times then takes the picture.

THE JOURNALIST: Would you allow me to sit on your bed? It's to get a better idea of the atmosphere.

ROLL: *(Getting up.)* Of course. You can even lie down on it.

THE JOURNALIST lies down on the bed, leaving one leg dangling of the side.

THE JOURNALIST: It's hard. What a genuine prison bed! Auw! *(He pulls his leg back up, rubs his ankle.)* Something bit me!

ROLL: Oh, I completely forgot about him. It's Rat-the-Bastard.

THE JOURNALIST: A rat!

ROLL: Yes. He's under the bed.

THE PHOTOGRAPHER: You want a picture of the rat?

THE JOURNALIST: Absolutely!

THE JOURNALIST gets up. THE PHOTOGRAPHER lies on the floor, looks under the bed, takes a picture with flash.

THE PHOTOGRAPHER: I don't know what that is going to give. I didn't see anything.

ROLL sits back on the bed.

THE JOURNALIST: Are you not afraid it will bite you?

ROLL: That he tries! It is trained, my rat.

THE JOURNALIST: *(Writing.)* It is trained.

BRIG bursts in.

BRIG: Gentlemen of the press! Quick, quick! My sincerest apologies … We got the cell wrong. It's not here. They are waiting for you next door.

THE JOURNALIST: What bad organisation. It's a scandal. I am scandalised!

THE PHOTOGRAPHER: Take this! I am leaving you your portraits. And your rat.

THE PHOTOGRAPHER pulls out of his camera a roll of film and throws it at ROLL's feet. THE JOURNALIST and THE PHOTOGRAPHER leave.)

BRIG: How could I have messed up like that? Anyway, not a word about this story, right, someone might regret it! Understood?

BRIG leaves, locks the door. RAT sticks his head out from under the bed.

RAT: And our Sir who took himself for someone he wasn't!
Sir gave his press conference! He let himself being
photographed in profile and full-face!

ROLL: Shut up!

MM BREDUMO: *(From the living room.)* Charles!

ROLL: Oh, the beard! *(To RAT.)* You, keep quiet.

ROLL puts his old man's mask back on and sits in the wheelchair.

SCENE THREE

MM BREDUMO, ROLL-BREDUMO

The living room. The room-prison isn't visible anymore.

MM BREDUMO: Chaaarles! Darling!

ROLL-BREDUMO enters in his wheelchair through the swing door.

ROLL-BREDUMO: What is going on? Why are you bothering
me? I'm in the middle of work.

MM BREDUMO: You were in your room? Why didn't you
answer? Were you asleep?

ROLL-BREDUMO: Are you asking me if I was asleep? That beats
everything! I work day and night. I am overworked, exhausted,
stressed out, I haven't closed my eyes in five days …

MM BREDUMO: Exactly, Charles …

ROLL-BREDUMO: And you dare to think that I am peacefully
having a nap in my room! That is just unbelievable.

MM BREDUMO: Charles, dear, you are so tired, let that not be
anything surprising.

ROLL-BREDUMO: On the other hand, if you think that I am
sleeping, having a rest for a moment, why do you wake me
up? That is just mental torture, that!

MM BREDUMO: I would never allow myself to disturb you,
Charles, but your mother is asking for you on the phone.

ROLL-BREDUMO: My mother? Ah, yes, Mum! Why didn't you
tell me immediately?

MM BREDUMO: I didn't have time for it.

ROLL-BREDUMO: *(On the phone.)* Here I am, Mummy. I let you wait. I am sorry. Excuse me. I am very well. Don't worry. But no, but no, come now. For you I always have time. You are so kind ... Yes, we'll come visit on Sunday ... What did I forget? Let me think ... No, I can't seem to ... Yes ... wait, wait ... But no, I didn't forget your birthday! How could I forget your birthday? ... How old? Thirty, I think. No, that's not possible! A hundred? Are you sure? ... Two wars and two revolutions. That's a well filled life ... A third one, what? You are kidding? ... Yes, you will live for a very, very long time still, dear Mummy, but there won't be any more wars, or revolutions in your life time ... You are sorry? You are sorry about what? ... Because you find it entertaining! ... Mum, you are talking nonsense ... We'll talk about all that on Sunday, at your place ... No, no, all is well ... So, sweet kisses ... Yes ... Me too, I love you too. *(He hangs up.)* Sweet Mummy. She will never change. *(To MM BREDUMO.)* On Sunday, we are invited to go to see Mum. It's her one hundredth birthday! What a woman!

MM BREDUMO: Yes. Admirable.

ROLL-BREDUMO: Well. I am going back to work. I have a report to do for the central Committee and I still have several files to look into. So, let nobody disturb me! Nobody! I'm not in. I am gone. I disappeared. I won't answer anymore!

MM BREDUMO: Very well, very well.

SCENE FOUR

ROLL, RAT, KEB

The room-prison.

When ROLL arrives, the room is empty. ROLL takes his mask off and lies on the bed. The door on the left opens. KEB falls on the wooden flooring, pushed by BRIG who closes the door. KEB is a small old man, badly shaven, his clothes are ripped. His face shows signs of punches. He gets up with difficulty, goes towards the can, spits then he sits against the wall, his head between his arms.

ROLL: Something wrong, old man?

KEB: My teeth. They broke my teeth.

ROLL: Come, sit down.

KEB: Thank you. *(He sits down on the bed, he cries.)*

ROLL: Have courage, my friend. Does it hurt that bad?

KEB: No, it doesn't hurt a lot. Not a lot. *(He goes to spit again. He returns and sits down. He cries.)*

RAT: *(From under the bed.)* Shut it!

KEB: What was that?

ROLL: *(Kicking with his foot under the bed.)* Nothing. That came from outside. *(Pause.)* They beat me too. And they will beat me again. But the truth is on our side and victory is near.

RAT: What a beautiful speech!

KEB: But what is …

ROLL: Nothing. Nothing. It's outside. Victory is near.

KEB: Victory?

ROLL: Yes, we are numerous. And the days of the tyrant are numbered

KEB: Tyrant?

ROLL: But, come on. Aren't you a political prisoner?

KEB: I am, yes, I am.

ROLL: Then you are one of us.

KEB: Who are they, these friends of yours?

ROLL: Well … the enemies of the government.

KEB: Of what government?

ROLL: The … of the … of course, the current government.

KEB: *(Standing up.)* Aha! So you are one of those brainless terrorists! One of those imbecile destructors! Those demagogue badmouths! Those rioting bastards! Those rabble rousing idiots! And I have to suffer your company! They throw me in the same cell! The horror! The shame!

RAT: What a shame!

ROLL: *(Kicks with his feet.)* What? How? Pardon? I didn't understand any of that.

KEB: Shut up! And if you could be kind enough not to talk to me anymore.

KEB spits in the can, sits on the floor with his back turned to ROLL.

ROLL: Why are you here, if you're not one of us?

KEB: Why? I don't know why. It must be a misunderstanding.

ROLL: Yes, so it seems, we really don't have anything to say to each other.

KEB sobs, ROLL turns towards the wall disgusted.

RAT: I can't stand it anymore! I can't stand it anymore!

ROLL: Silence, Rat!

RAT crawls from under the bed, he dusts himself off. KEB, dumbfounded, looks at him.

RAT: I had enough of your story, I'm going. *(He knocks at the door.)* Brig! Hey, Brig! I want to leave!

BRIG: *(From outside.)* Nobody leaves. Those that are inside, stay inside.

KEB: *(To RAT.)* Hey! You there! Who are you?

RAT turns to KEB, balancing on the tips of his toes, hands in his pocket.

RAT: Guess!

ROLL: It's Rat-the-bastard. A childhood friend of mine.

RAT: That's it. That's it.

ROLL: He follows me everywhere. Even here. So, I hid him under the bed. *(To RAT.)* You did promise me to keep quiet.

RAT: I had enough of hearing all your nonsense. What were you talking about?

KEB: None of your business! It's our story. Why did you come here?

RAT: I was told that we could have a nice evening together, Roll and me. I didn't know you were going to be here. And I am so bored, all alone in my cell.

KEB: What cell?

RAT: Death row.

KEB: You are sentenced to death?

RAT: As everyone.

KEB: You're playing with words. How did you manage to leave your cell?

RAT: Through the little holes. Disguised as a rat, you pass unnoticed. *(He shows his mask.)*

KEB: *(To ROLL.)* He's mad, your friend. What is he talking about?

ROLL: He likes to play around. But he's not a bad bloke.

RAT: I only ask to spend the evening with you two.

KEB: But we talk about serious things, and you interrupt us all the time. You can stay under one condition: you are going to sit down and you will keep quiet.

RAT takes a chair and sits down.

RAT: Keep quiet. Keep quiet … Can I smoke at least?

KEB: If they left you your cigarettes.

RAT: Why would they have taken them from me?

KEB: That's what happens in prisons.

RAT: *(Lighting a cigarette.)* He calls this a prison!

KEB: Come on. Where were we? I forgot where I was. Ah, yes!

KEB starts to cry again. ROLL lies back on the bed. RAT covers his ears.

SCENE FIVE

ROLL, KEB, RAT

The room-prison.

ROLL: Will you stop crying! You're not a man!

KEB: You are too young to understand that a man can cry as well. I am not at all ashamed of my tears. They are not tears of weakness. Neither do I cry over my physical pains. They are tears of sadness and despair.

ROLL: And what is the cause of this sadness and despair? The loss of your last rotten teeth, perhaps?

RAT: *(Flicking his cigarette butt.)* A nice evening!

KEB: Silence! *(To ROLL.)* You're laughing at me. I don't care.

ROLL: Then talk.

KEB: Yes, maybe that would be good for you. *(Sighs.)* Do you know who beat me?

ROLL: The same bastard who beats everyone around here, I guess.

RAT: I bet it's Brig. Good old Brig, so conscientious.

KEB: That man is my best friend.

RAT: Congratulations!

KEB: That man was more than a friend to me, more than a brother. And today, he beat me. He threw in my face: 'Traitor' While he knows I am innocent! Would twenty years of friendship not be enough to know each other? Twenty years of working together outside the law.

ROLL: I'm beginning to understand. This highly respectable man, who keeps himself busy with knocking out teeth throughout the day, was your friend outside the law.

RAT: I bet it's that good old bastard Brig.

ROLL: You have dreamed together, you fought, suffered together.

KEB: One day, a long time ago, when we hadn't taken power yet, they arrested me. It was after a protest march we had organised, him and me. They took me. They beat me. I didn't cry, it was enemies that beat me. They wanted to know who the other organisers were. They tortured me. I didn't talk.

ROLL: It was worth it.

KEB: Yes, it was worth it. I was proud of myself. I was in prison for three years. So was he, but later on. Oh, he was incredible! One day, he risked his life to save me.

RAT yawns loudly. Angry look from KEB.

RAT: I didn't say anything.

KEB: We had to blow up a bridge. I didn't have time to get away. I hurt my head. I couldn't move …

RAT: Yes, yes, we know. And he saved your life by risking his. We've heard that one before.

KEB: Please be quiet!

RAT: Do you really care about this subject of conversation?

KEB: Of course I care about it. But I had enough of you, so will you please leave immediately!

RAT: *(Getting up.)* I'd happily go, believe me. I'm bored here. But it isn't that simple. Brig, the guard, doesn't want to open up. Those that are inside, stay inside, he said.

KEB: Do I care about the guard! I can make you disappear when I want to. You're just a fruit of my imagination. I only have to stop thinking about you and you don't exist anymore.

RAT: Ah, yes? Try then.

RAT takes a chair and sits in front of KEB. They look at each other.

RAT: It looks like I am still here.

KEB: My God! What is going on?

RAT: What is going on is that even though I am a fruit of your imagination, it's from your involuntary imagination that I am the fruit. The fruit. Ha ha. That's a good one! The fruit! *(He approaches KEB.)* What I mean to say is that you didn't deliberately imagine me. I didn't come from here *(He taps the forehead of KEB.)*, but from there *(He taps the back of KEB's head.)* Here, *(Taps the forehead.)* are the fruits, ha, ha, you can command, and there *(Taps the back of the head.)* are the fruits that move by themselves.

ROLL: *(To RAT.)* Don't jostle him about. Look in what state you got him!

(To KEB.) Lie down on the bed. Rest for a moment.

KEB: *(Lying down.)* Yes, I am feeling very dizzy. Nothing is going as it should.

RAT: You want to pass an evening in the company of Roll. There he is. But he's not alone. He is never alone. I follow him everywhere.

(KEB snores.)

ROLL: Poor old man. He is already asleep.

RAT: Good. We can finally talk about something else than politics.

ROLL: But it is very interesting! This old man has sacrificed his life for an ideal and now sees that it was in vain: his comrades became torturers, and he himself their victim. And he still believes in his ideal. He hangs on to it. Don't you think that's bizarre? He should have lost faith …

KEB: Ah, no! So, my whole life was just a mistake then?

RAT: Aren't you asleep, old man?

KEB: I sleep, but I am also listening. I will never forsake my beliefs. The ideas for which I sacrificed youth, family! *(He gets up.)* I killed for my ideals, sir. I did filthy things for my ideals, I did everything, yes. I would have betrayed my mother for it; I would have sold my children. If I had any.

RAT: Bravo, bravo. That's really something to boast about.

ROLL: Calm down, calm down.

KEB: Calm down? And now they ask me to renounce all that? At seventy years old, they would ask me that? Even if Brig beat me, it proves nothing.

RAT: I knew it was him.

KEB: It proves only that Brig is mistaken. That he thinks I am guilty, and that he does his job. People can be wrong, but the Party, never! *(He lies down again.)*

RAT: He thinks he's on stage, my word! Old liar. Well, there's nothing we can do with him anymore. But you, you should understand. His experience should help you.

ROLL: Me? The blunder of that unfortunate wreck can't teach me anything at all.

RAT: When you are seventy, you will be in the same situation. Your people will be in power, and they will break your teeth. *(He points out KEB.)* You don't see then that it's you? What you will be in forty years?

ROLL: Me? That?

RAT: Yes. And you know it very well.

MM BREDUMO: *(From the living-room.)* Chaaarles! Darling!

SCENE SIX

ROLL-BREDUMO, MM BREDUMO

ARGAS, MM ARGAS

The living room.

ARGAS and MM ARGAS are sitting in armchairs; before them on the low table, glasses. MM BREDUMO stands close to the door of the room.

MM BREDUMO: Darling!

ROLL-BREDUMO arrives in his wheel chair. He comes to a halt when he sees that there are visitors.

ROLL-BREDUMO: *(Aside to MM BREDUMO.)* No! You can't do that to me! Why did you invite them?

MM BREDUMO: I didn't invite them. They came by unexpectedly.

ARGAS: We are disturbing. I can see we are disturbing him.

MM BREDUMO: Not at all. It will do him good to stop for a while. He has been working for hours.

ROLL-BREDUMO: For hours? You're joking. *(While coming closer.)* Hello, Argas. Hello, dear Madame. *(Handshakes.)*

ARGAS: We are disturbing you. I am sorry.

MM ARGAS: Charles is always happy to see me. Aren't you, Charles?

ROLL-BREDUMO: Happy, is too little said, dear Madame. I am elated.

MM BREDUMO: A glass of mineral water, darling?

ROLL-BREDUMO: Whisky, straight.

MM BREDUMO: You are not going to work anymore today?

ROLL-BREDUMO: First you tell me: you work for hours and hours, and now: you are not going to work anymore today?

ARGAS: We are disturbed him. It's our fault. He won't be able to work anymore if he has a drink.

ROLL-BREDUMO: One glass! I have one glass, and they make a drama out of it.

MM ARGAS: You must have so much work with all these arrests.

ARGAS: Darling, please.

ROLL-BREDUMO: What arrests?

MM ARGAS: But, come on! It's not a secret.

ROLL-BREDUMO: Ah, no?

ARGAS: Martha!

MM ARGAS: But, come on! The whole world knows about it.

ROLL-BREDUMO: Oh, really?

MM ARGAS: Yes, of course. They talk about nothing else.

ROLL-BREDUMO: About what then?

MM ARGAS: But … of … the purification. The arrests, the disappearances …

ROLL-BREDUMO: Well, well. And the whole world talks about it?

ARGAS: Charles!   Don't listen to Martha. She says just about anything.

ROLL-BREDUMO: Noemi, I'd like another drink. *(Mm Bredumo serves him.)*

ARGAS: Charles, I have come because I am terribly worried.

ROLL-BREDUMO: Come, come, my dear Argas.

ARGAS: You think I shouldn't be worried, Charles?

ROLL-BREDUMO: If you don't have anything to reproach yourself for ...

MM ARGAS: Oh no! Ernest certainly has nothing to reproach himself for ...

ARGAS: This ... Zaik ... he who worked with us ...

ROLL-BREDUMO: Go on?

ARGAS: Is ... is he really guilty?

ROLL-BREDUMO: If they arrested him ...

ARGAS: But you, Charles, you were his friend ... Do you think he's guilty?

ROLL-BREDUMO: What difference does that make, what I think?

(Silence. MM BREDUMO fills the glasses.)

MM BREDUMO: Charles was in prison, in his youth.

MM ARGAS: Oh, tell us! That must be so interesting!

ROLL-BREDUMO: Yes, it was extremely amusing.

ARGAS: You suffered for your political ideas under the old regime. How beautiful.

MM BREDUMO: Yes, it was beautiful, our youth. And Charles wrote poems.

MM ARGAS: Love poems? Oh, I would so love to read them!

MM BREDUMO: We lost them. And we forgot them.

MM ARGAS: What a shame! You could have published them now. I adore poetry! Ernest, unfortunately, is so mundane. He would be absolutely incapable of writing even one single verse. And he never went to prison.

ROLL-BREDUMO: Now that is so unromantic, unforgiveable, in fact. But maybe it is still not too late.

ARGAS: You are joking, I hope.

ROLL-BREDUMO: Of course. Now, if you would excuse me. I have a few urgent phone calls to make. I will join you again in a few moments.

SCENE SEVEN

BRIG, ROLL, RAT, KEB

The room-prison.

ROLL arrives from the living room. He gets rid of his mask. The other characters are finishing a game of cards. On the floor are two empty bottles of wine.

KEB: That's weird. It's always me who's paying.

RAT: Because it's always you who loses.

KEB: But that's just what's weird. I had good cards.

RAT: You don't know how to play. Good cards are not always enough.

KEB gives money to BRIG.

KEB: The same again.

BRIG: This is not enough.

KEB: That's the price.

BRIG: And the tax? It's dangerous what I am doing here. It's not allowed. I'm risking my position.

RAT: You already had your tax with those first two bottles. Now, you are going to bring wine without tax and without discussion. And hurry up!

BRIG: What a bastard, that Rat! He would rip your shirt off. *(He leaves.)*

RAT: *(To KEB.)* You let yourself do.

KEB: What do you want? He does what he wants around here. *(He feels his jaw.)*

RAT: I wonder how much he would charge to bring us a girl.

ROLL: You are not thinking about that!

RAT: On the contrary. I think of nothing else. We could share the cost.

KEB: No, I'm out. I'm not giving a penny.

RAT: In that case, you will keep your eyes closed, old man.

ROLL: I never paid for a girl.

RAT: You think a girl would come all the way here, just for your beautiful eyes? You forget where we are.

ROLL: I have absolutely no desire to have a girl.

RAT: I always thought that there was something wrong with you.

ROLL: Not at all. It is simply that, I am in love.

RAT: That doesn't make any difference.

ROLL: It does. For me, it does.

RAT: Alright. Alright. I'll pay for her alone.

KEB: *(Lying down on the bed.)* I'm going to sleep.

RAT: Keep your ideals warm.

> *BRIG enters with two bottles of wine and glasses. KEB shows interest. BRIG distributes the glasses, and pours.*

BRIG: I even brought glasses. For free. To our health.

RAT: To our loves. *(They drink.)*

BRIG: Actually, I was going to propose to you … *(He whispers in RAT's ear.)*

RAT: Now, now. How curious. But I don't think anyone feels like it.

BRIG: It's not expensive. *(Whispers.)* With the risk that I'm running …

RAT: That's not cheap. Is she any good at least? How old?

BRIG: Twenty. A beauty.

RAT: *(Giving money to BRIG)* Deal. Hurry up.

BRIG: It's as if she was already here. *(He leaves.)*

RAT: That's fantastic. He just came to offer me one.

ROLL: Offer you what?

RAT: An idealist, to keep us company.

KEB: I did the black market, but that, I never sold.

RAT: You missed out on something.

ROLL: *(To KEB.)* You sold on the black market? But that's maybe why you are in here.

KEB: Of course. It's not for no reason.

ROLL: Then why do you play the innocent?

KEB: Everyone plays the innocent when they're defeated. With Brig however, that's pointless. He was there.

ROLL: Where?

KEB: On the black market. We worked together.

ROLL: But he, he's a free man!

KEB: Of course. I didn't give him up. It's him who will get me out of here.

RAT: Count on that!

ROLL: But he beat you!

KEB: For form's sake.

ROLL: And your teeth?

KEB: I already had dentures, see.

ROLL: That's enlightening.

KEB: You haven't seen anything yet, son. Wherever you go, it's the same.

ROLL: And your past, as fellow fighters?

KEB: We made one up, a past, with Brig of course. You can easily make up a past.

ROLL: That's very, very enlightening.

RAT: Don't turn your nose up, you! Don't be all wide eyed! The wide eyes, you don't know them, by accident? You never heard about them?

ROLL: Shut up!

RAT: It is not in my habit to keep quiet when I have something to say.

ROLL: It doesn't stop me from having my political convictions.

RAT: Only, that is not why you are in prison. Nobody is interested in your political convictions, nobody gives a damn.

KEB: Eh, eh, that's good that! Well then, young man! So it's for the use and sale of narcotics? And he acts like the great revolutionary! Eh, eh.

ROLL: Enough, old man. You're hurting my ears.

RAT: Let's drink rather. *(He pours into everyone's glasses.)*

ROLL: *(Raising his glass.)* It is time to drink because there is no one left to clear the unending fields of melancholy.
The shadows have entered the room
The silence becomes dark
Alone the hearts beat as fists
Knocking on the door.

ROLL drinks. KEB snores.

RAT: Are you high or what?

ROLL: Yesterday, everything was more beautiful
The music in the trees
The wind in my hair
And in your outstretched hands
There was sunlight …

Enter BRIG.

SCENE EIGHT

ROLL, RAT, KEB, BRIG, NOEMI

The room-prison.

BRIG: It is not allowed to recite poetry.

RAT: Where is she?

BRIG: *(Letting NOEMI in.)* Here she is.

ROLL: Noemi!

NOEMI: Roll! *(She throws herself into ROLL's arms.)*

ROLL: You? Here?

RAT: You see? You should have chipped in.

ROLL: This is unbelievable! This is horrible!

ROLL pushes NOEMI away and throws himself on the bed, which wakes KEB up.

KEB: What's going on? Can't a man sleep anymore? Is the interval over? Is it my wife calling me again?

NOEMI: *(Covering her face.)* I'm ashamed, I'm ashamed.

RAT: This is not the time. And it's a bit late. Come! *(He takes NOEMI by the arm.)*

NOEMI: Leave me alone!

NOEMI tries to leave, but BRIG pushes her towards RAT.

BRIG: He paid. What's wrong with you? It's not the first time you come here.

NOEMI: Roll!

ROLL puts himself between NOEMI and RAT.

ROLL: Leave her alone!

RAT: Pay me back, then!

ROLL: *(Taking money from his pocket.)* How much?

RAT: One fifty.

ROLL: I haven't got enough. *(To BRIG.)* Give him his money back!

BRIG: I'm not crazy. Besides, I only have half. She has the other half.

ROLL: *(To NOEMI.)* Give him his money back!

NOEMI: I don't have it anymore.

BRIG: She lying! She has it! I just gave it to her.

ROLL: Give that money back, Noemi!

KEB: She's not crazy!

NOEMI: I need it darling. Really need it. It's to buy myself drugs. *(She clings to ROLL.)*

ROLL: No!

ROLL pushes NOEMI off and punches RAT.

RAT: You don't really want to fight for her? With me?

Another punch from ROLL. RAT returns the punch. A fight. BRIG tries to separate them. NOEMI screams, KEB drinks from the bottle. ROLL ends up flat out on the floor. NOEMI looks after him.

MM BREDUMO: *(From the living room.)* Chaaarles!

RAT: *(To KEB.)* They're calling you.

KEB: *(Drinking.)* No way. You go.

RAT shrugs his shoulders, disguises himself as BREDUMO and sits down in the wheelchair.

SCENE NINE

ARGAS, MM ARGAS

MM BREDUMO, RAT-BREDUMO

The living room

The ARGAS' are eating. MM BREDUMO stands by the door of the room.

ARGAS: These are excellent.

MM ARGAS: I prefer salmon.

MM BREDUMO: Darling!

RAT-BREDUMO arrives in his wheelchair.

MM BREDUMO: I am sorry Charles. I was forced to wake you up. We could hear you snoring up to here.

RAT-BREDUMO: You must be having hallucinations. What? Are they still here?

MM BREDUMO: I am afraid so!

RAT-BREDUMO: And you gave them something to eat! That beats all! You do everything to keep them here.

MM BREDUMO: Oh no, Charles! I told them that it was George's day off, so they ordered a small cold buffet over the phone.

RAT-BREDUMO: The nerve! Are they going to bring their bed here as well?

MM ARGAS: You must be hungry, Charles. Come and taste these delicious stuffed avocados.

RAT-BREDUMO: I would like something to drink, Noemi.

MM BREDUMO: You don't think you had enough to drink already?

RAT-BREDUMO: How do you want me to put up with them, without a drink?

(MM BREDUMO and RAT-BREDUMO join the ARGAS'.)

MM ARGAS: When I eat nice things, I always think of those who are hungry.

RAT-BREDUMO: That is extremely generous from you, dear Madame. *(He drinks.)*

MM ARGAS: Hunger in the world in general, and in our country in particular, is a burning topic.

ARGAS: Change the subject, Marthe! You'll make us loose our appetite.

MM ARGAS: It has the exact opposite effect on me. It makes me want to eat even more. I do have to keep an eye on my figure though.

RAT-BREDUMO: How right you are, dear Madame! It is of the utmost importance to keep that figure of a young girl.

MM ARGAS: Flatterer! *(To MM BREDUMO.)* Aren't you jealous, Noemi?

MM BREDUMO: Jealous? Ah, yes, of course, a little. But at our age, you know …

MM ARGAS: I still find Charles terribly attractive.

RAT-BREDUMO: And I find my wife more and more attractive. You know, age has nothing to do with it. My mother didn't stop becoming lovelier right up until the day she died.

MM BREDUMO: Your mother isn't dead yet, Charles.

RAT-BREDUMO: No. She is only a hundred years old. She called me today.

General silence.

RAT-BREDUMO: *(Holding his glass towards MM BREDUMO.)* Please, Noemi.

MM BREDUMO: Are you sure, Charles?

RAT-BREDUMO: Of what? Sure of what?

MM BREDUMO: Alright, alright. Here. *(She fills his glass.)*

ARGAS: What's so annoying about those starving people, is that they take themselves for the ruling class. As if it is easy to run a country!

MM ARGAS: If we belong to the ruling class, it is because of our work, our intelligence, and above all, our devotion to the Party.

ARGAS: It's true. It is absolutely true what you say about our devotion to the Party. What is difficult in exercising power, is the education of the people. They're lazy. They don't work. They don't educate themselves ...

MM ARGAS: All they can do is shout in the street and strike. That they work a bit more and make a few less children!

RAT-BREDUMO: But how, dear Madame, how would you stop them making so many children?

ARGAS: That's another question of education.

MM ARGAS: Yes. Give them some pills or sterilize them, if they like it or not.

RAT-BREDUMO: That's a brilliant idea that! *(To ARGAS.)* Politically, your wife is very evolved, Argas. Almost as much as you. And she expresses herself in an incomparable fashion.

ARGAS: Doesn't she? She has her opinion on any subject.

RAT-BREDUMO: She is incomparable!

MM ARGAS: The important thing isn't, to have or not to have a handful of rice ...

RAT-BREDUMO: The important thing, is that ...

MM BREDUMO: No, Charles!

MM ARGAS: What's important is to keep your head high during misery.

RAT-BREDUMO: Provided that you have your mouth open, seagull droppings ...

MM BREDUMO: Now Charles!

RAT-BREDUMO: Why? It's very nourishing.

MM ARGAS: Life has taught me many things. Mind you, I was raised in Switzerland, during the war …

RAT-BREDUMO: The last war, in Switzerland? You weren't even born!

MM ARGAS: I am talking about the last world war.

RAT-BREDUMO: Ah, the war of the others!

MM ARGAS: We had some very tough privations, very severe, unsupportable rations, in Switzerland. But nobody complained.

RAT-BREDUMO: That's the grandeur of spirit, guaranty Swiss made! Do they export it to less advantaged countries?

MM BREDUMO: Charles, you had too much to drink.

RAT-BREDUMO: Not enough yet. Pour!

MM BREDUMO: You shouldn't drink anymore, Charles!

RAT-BREDUMO: I am an adult. *(He pours himself a drink.)*

MM BREDUMO: I'm sorry. I think I'll put him to bed.

MM ARGAS: I find him so charming like this. So delicious. I have never seen him like this.

ARGAS: Darling, it's late. We should go home.

MM ARGAS: I feel so good. And we had such an interesting conversation.

RAT-BREDUMO: Oh, yes, Madame! You have taught me extraordinary things! You have opened the doors to wells so deep … so dark …

An embarrassed silence. BREDUMO is completely drunk.

MM BREDUMO: Wells generally don't have doors, my darling.

RAT-BREDUMO: Wells don't have doors? But there! *(He points to the door in the back.)* There's one! A door!

He lifts himself up a bit from his chair, still pointing to the door.

RAT-BREDUMO: A door to exit! Leave! Out!

He crashes the glasses on the table.

MM BREDUMO: Charles! Excuse him! I'm so very sorry.

ARGAS and MM ARGAS retreat towards the door in the back. MM BREDUMO accompanies them. They leave. RAT-BREDUMO throws an empty bottle against the closed door.

RAT-BREDUMO: And keep your head high! And keep that figure!

SCENE TEN

ROLL, NOEMI, KEB, RAT

The room-prison.

NOEMI is still leaning over ROLL. KEB lies asleep on the bed. RAT arrives. He takes the mask off and places it on KEB's face. He helps KEB up and sits him into the wheelchair.

RAT: *(To KEB.)* I got rid of your friends.

KEB: Thank you. Thank you very much, young man.

RAT: *(To NOEMI.)* We're off.

KEB: *(Pointing to ROLL.)* Is he dead?

RAT: No more than ourselves. *(He knocks on the door.)* Open up, Brig! It's over. *(The door opens.)*

NOEMI goes towards KEB, kisses him on the forehead.

NOEMI: Sleep well, Charles.

RAT: *(To NOEMI.)* Help me.

RAT takes ROLL by the shoulders. NOEMI lifts up ROLL's feet.

RAT: Well then, good night!

KEB: Farewell.

RAT and NOEMI leave carrying ROLL.

SCENE ELEVEN

KEB (BREDUMO), BRIG (GEORGES)

The room.

BRIG enters dressed as a valet.

BRIG: Would Sir like to go to sleep?

KEB: Yes, George. I feel very tired.

BRIG: Nothing surprising there, Sir.

KEB: I think I have also ... drunk a little.

BRIG: Sufficient, I believe, Sir.

BRIG removes the board and prepares the bed. He returns the table and the chairs to their place. He unrolls the carpet, hangs the pictures back on the wall, as the curtain on the window and the door. He helps KEB to take off his old clothing under which he wears pyjamas. He helps KEB to his bed.

KEB: It's a shame they're gone.

BRIG: The Argas'? But it was you who ...

KEB: No. I'm talking about those that were here, in my room.

BRIG: There was nobody here. It was just a game, a dream.

KEB: I know, I know. There is one thing that intrigues me, George. Who is Rat? Who was Rat?

BRIG: With the respect that I owe you, Sir, Rat-the-bastard is yourself, Sir. That is to say, what you were in your youth.

KEB: Impossible, George. I was Roll, the young idealist poet.

BRIG: That is not completely inaccurate. The truth is that you were both at the same time. Roll, the idealist, and Rat-the-bastard, the cynic and, forgive me, rather shameless.

KEB: I can't believe that. I have no memory at all of such a character.

BRIG: You have eliminated from your memory all that was disagreeable to you. You indulged in imagining yourself with the flattering traits of this young man Roll, the image itself of enthusiasm and purity. On the other hand, the less pleasing side of Sir's character was, if I dare to say, passed into oblivion. Nothing surprising there. Time embellishes memories.

KEB: Can you prove that, George?

BRIG: Nothing is easier. At the time, to us, you always were Rat-the-bastard. Besides, the presence of that young man this evening, here, should suffice to convince you. Despite yourself, it has surfaced from the deepest of your memories.

KEB: So, at the time, you called me Rat-the-bastard? I didn't know that.

BRIG: Only when you weren't there, Sir.

KEB: Behind my back, no?

BRIG: Of course. Otherwise, you'd be hurt. Your Roll-the-poet side was very sensitive.

KEB: Damned Brig!

BRIG: Sir?

KEB: Call me Keb, okay. Tonight we'll go right to the end of the game.

BRIG: As Sir desires. But what do you understand under 'to the end of the game?'

KEB: Just that, that we won't play it anymore. No more Sir, and no more George. Like at the time, on the black market.

BRIG: All that is in the past. Times have changed a lot since then.

KEB: But we, we haven't changed, Brig.

BRIG: We did, we've changed a lot. Sir has become Sir and I have become George, Sir's chamber valet.

KEB: Admit you'd have to be pretty smart to manage that.

BRIG: Especially from Sir's part, considering his situation. You really are Rat-the-bastard!

KEB: When I think of it ... that Rat ... on final account, I find him fantastic.

BRIG: I would never have become the valet of just about anyone. Only, Sir started to take himself seriously, and he started to take me as his room valet for real.

KEB: Forgive me, Brig. I forgot sometimes, it's true. But it is truly over. Are we still friends?

BRIG: Of course, my old Keb. And we will have a drink.

BRIG brings two glasses and a bottle to the table, next to the bed. He sits down on a chair close by.

BRIG: To our health, Keb!

KEB: To our youth! To Rat-the-bastard! *(They drink.)*

BRIG: Do we also drink to our future?

KEB: We don't have one, Brig. We are old.

BRIG: Not that old.

KEB: No, not that old, but …

BRIG: Is there something else?

KEB: Yes, Brig. Tomorrow … From tomorrow … I have to sign the sentence of about a hundred people.

Silence.

KEB: And I have to sentence a dozen of them to death. It's the required percentage.

Silence.

BRIG: So?

KEB: They are innocent, Brig. They are all innocent. I know.

BRIG: The whole world knows. So?

KEB: I don't want to do it. I can't.

BRIG: Someone else will do it.

KEB: That's not an excuse.

BRIG: Absolutely not.

Silence.

KEB: I'm thinking of Roll. He would never do something like that.

BRIG: That's where you are mistaken. Roll would do it. With a calm conscience. In the name of his ideal. It's dangerous, people who have ideals. It's the worst of all races. They are capable of everything and anything.

KEB: So, you think Roll would do it?

BRIG: Yes. But one person I know, who wouldn't do it is Rat-the-bastard. You couldn't make him accept that it was for the good of everyone and for the triumph of the Cause. No, you couldn't make him. I am sure of that.

KEB: Me too. I am sure. Roll is dead. I am Rat-the-bastard. Give me a drink. *(He drinks.)* I would prefer to be amongst the victims.

BRIG: Is that what you tried to imagine in the skin of the old man?

KEB: Yes, but sadly, I'm not the poor old Keb. I am the old but powerful Bredumo, who holds in his hands the lot of about a hundred of his equals.

BRIG: Powerful? Ha! Ha! You are less powerful than an earth worm, or the lowest of tramps. The power is somewhere else. You are but the murder weapon. Your only power is to refuse obedience, and there is only one way to do that. One only.

BRIG takes a small packet from his pocket and empties it in KEB's glass.

KEB: My dear Brig. What luck that you stayed with me! Is it quick?

BRIG: It's instant. And painless. I am very happy that you agree, Keb.

KEB: And if I didn't?

BRIG: I would have made you drink it without you knowing it. I would have been forced to, because of our friendship, you understand?

KEB: I understand. Give me the glass. And you, what will become of you?

BRIG: Let Sir not worry about me. I will engage myself as a prison guard. I can be useful down there. In prison, there are always a lot of good people.

KEB empties his glass and gives it to BRIG.

KEB: Good night, Brig. It's good wine, very good wine.

BRIG: Yes, very good.

KEB: You will tell my mother ... you will tell the truth ... and Noemi. They will understand.

BRIG: Yes.

Silence. BRIG leans over KEB. He walks away from the bed. He sniffs. He looks around him.

BRIG: God! I forgot the can!

He leaves with the can. Curtain.

End of play.

Neuchatel, 1984 (Original Version, 1972).

THE GREY HOUR
OR THE LAST CLIENT

Characters

SHE

HE

THE MUSICIAN

A room.

Stuffed with a large bed, a table, chairs, a wind screen, a coat hanger, a sink, a stove, dirty dishes, empty bottles, etc. Next to the bed, a bedside lamp. In the back, a window, through which enters a little light from the street. To the right a door.

The room is empty, lit only by the window.

Nostalgic music comes from the neighbouring room. (A violin.)

Scene One

Where they talk about death and the future

The sound of a key in the lock. The music stops.

A woman of an indefinable age enters. SHE is violently made up, has her hair too blonde, wears a figure hugging dress, shoes with the heels too high, with which she has difficulty walking. A worn fur shawl on her shoulders, hand bag, a cigarette holder between her lips.

SHE is followed by a man of a certain age, not very tall, almost bald, who carries a bottle.

SHE closes the door of the room, hangs her bag over the back of a chair, throws her shawl on the bed, lights the lamp. HE puts the bottle on the table, takes his overcoat and hat off, hangs them on the coat hanger. HE sits in front of the bed, takes some bank notes out of his pocket, arranges them carefully on the table.

SHE busies herself, rinses glasses, takes two to the table. SHE sits on the bed, takes her shoes off, massages her feet. HE fills the two glasses, brings one to the woman. HE returns to his seat.

SHE: Oh, my feet ... *(She rubs her hands.)* And my fingers ... completely frozen.

HE: Always your hands and feet! Always frozen! What's it going to be like when it's winter?

SHE: I can't think of it. *(Pause.)* It's nice in here.

HE: What more do you want?

SHE: Apparently. *(They drink.)* And you? How are you?

HE: Are you asking me? How dare you?

SHE: You asked me more than enough, no? It's my turn.

HE: It's not your turn.

SHE: Oh really, why?

HE: Because I'm the one who's paying. You have no right to ask questions to the one who is paying.

SHE: Ah! *(They drink.)* You haven't been for a long time.

HE: So what? You missed me maybe?

SHE: No, but I wondered …

HE: Stop wondering.

SHE: You got picked up again?

HE: Picked up? What do you mean?

SHE: Caught red handed?

HE: None of your business.

SHE: No. Was it long?

HE: What?

SHE: Your stay in prison.

HE: Shut up! *(They drink.)*

SHE: Each time I don't hear from you for a long time, I wonder if you are in prison, or if you are dead. Do you realise, if you were dead, they wouldn't even let me know.

HE: Yes, and you'd wait for me downstairs every evening, for years. You'd go just as far as the cafe, you'd return to the corner of the street … By the morning, you'd be tired, you'd go back up. But you couldn't sleep. *(Dreaming.)* You will open the window, you will look down the street. You will listen to the sound of the steps in the street, in the hallway. You will look for an object that reminds you of how I take my coat off. But I didn't forget anything at your place. *(Pause.)* When the sun comes up, you close the window, you go to bed. Like that, for years, everyday.

Music comes from the neighbouring room. A few broken-off chords, as a sob, ending in comical hiccups.

SHE: *(Theatrical.)* And one evening the silence will be dark as in the lonely gardens of childhood; and one evening the moon will wander over the roofs of the city; another time the wind will enter through the open window with the scent of damp earth; and another night the rain will lash against the windows, and it will seem to me then that the drops are my own tears. And there will be winter nights with snowflakes swirling around the streetlamp, and those nights will be the loneliest, because they will bring me the certainty of your death.

HE: *(Quickly wiping away a tear with a finger.)* Like that, for years.

SHE: You would think so. You don't have to cry, you're still here.

HE: Eh? What are you saying? I drank too much. *(He drinks.)*

SHE: Does our future depend on that?

HE: What? Did you say our future?

SHE: Yes, I did. I wasn't thinking.

HE: You'd do better to think.

SHE: I don't know what to think anymore.

HE: Of our future.

SHE: Usually, I don't have to think of our future.

HE: Usually, what do you have to think of?

SHE: Of what? Of nothing. Usually, they don't ask me to think.

HE: What do they ask you?

SHE: Other stuff.

HE: Why?

SHE: Why? *(They drink.)*

HE: What were we talking about earlier? I forgot the previous question.

SHE: What question?

HE: The question coming before your question, I forgot it.

SHE: Ah! You too?

HE: I remember!

SHE: Good sign.

HE: I … re … memmmm … beuh …

SHE: Impossible! Before, you never remembered. So now that you are completely wasted …

HE: Shit! And shit and shit! You made me loose the thread!

SHE: I didn't do it on purpose.

HE: No, no. You didn't do it on purpose. As usual.

Scene Two

With drawn knife

HE gets up. Slowly HE pulls a switchblade out of his pocket. HE opens it, admires it. With dance steps, HE walks up to the bed, holds the knife up.

SHE: Is that for me?

Music. A few short chords, strong, dramatic. SHE screams.

HE: What's wrong with you?

SHE: I was scared.

HE: Of my knife?

SHE: No. Of the music.

HE: What music? I didn't hear any music. *(HE lowers the knife, looks at it sadly.)* And my knife?

SHE: What about your knife?

HE: It doesn't scare you?

SHE: Why would it scare me?

HE: Because it cuts.

SHE: All knifes cut. If all knifes scared me … I wouldn't even dare making myself a sandwich, would I.

HE: You're showing off.

SHE: No, I ask myself questions.

HE: About me?

SHE: About knives. Why would I be scared of them?

HE: Because it's death, or something close anyway. You're not scared?

SHE: OK, OK, if you insist ... I am very scared. Let's move on.

HE: Not like that! *(HE returns to his seat.)*

SHE: How than?

HE: I don't know. Something different ... I don't know. Find something!

SHE: I'm sleepy.

HE: That's not part of the game. Drink! *(HE pours the glasses, they drink.)* Make something up!

SHE: Make something up? Like what?

HE: Anything! Anything! Make something up!

SHE: OK, don't get excited. I'll make something up.

Scene Three

The dawn in all its splendour

HE: Right, go!

SHE: *(Making it up.)* The evening, I was feeling sleepy ... As I was in the morning, for that matter. *(SHE lets herself fall on the bed.)* Truth be said, I'm always sleepy.

HE: Is that all? *(Lifts his knife.)*

SHE: No, no. And I had dreams. But not anymore.

HE: Not anymore? I want you to dream right now!

SHE: I cannot dream on command.

HE: Yes, you can. Or else ... *(HE lifts his knife.)*

SHE: OK, OK. I'll dream you something.

HE: Something real?

SHE: Yes. Well, something touching on reality.

HE: I don't want realities.

SHE: You're so tiring. OK then, something touching on a dream.

HE: Dreams about what?

SHE: I don't know. I don't dream about whatever I want.

HE: No, about what I want, me.

SHE: Oh really? So, then I'll dream about what the gentleman would like my daydream to be about.

HE: Dream about us. About me and you.

SHE: That's going to end badly..

HE: Meaning what?

SHE: I wonder what that will give.

HE: Try anyway.

SHE: OK. *(SHE closes her eyes.)* I'm on a hill and they ...

HE: And me?

SHE: I'm not seeing you yet. They're violating me.

HE: See me immediately, without that ... *(HE lifts his knife.)*

SHE: Yes. It's 'without that', I am seeing you immediately. You are my saviour.

HE: Good!

SHE: You come up to me, you chase the others, you take me in your arms ... Dawn breaks in all its splendour.

HE: That's good.

SHE: It's wonderful. *(SHE dozes off.)*

HE: That's a pretty good find. And after that? *(Screaming.)* And after that?

SHE: *(Jumps.)* After what?

HE: When I break out in all my splendour ...

SHE: You? In all your splendour?

HE: Yes, you said that.

SHE: I must have gotten it wrong.

HE: I recommend you don't get it wrong again.

SHE: No? Okay. So dawn breaks, the others have gone, you come up to me and in turn you rape me.

HE: That's not a dream!

SHE: No. You're a pile of shite.

HE: That your last word?

SHE: That's my last word.

Scene Four

An infinite sadness

HE: Here, have another drink.

SHE: I can't really drink to infinity. *(Pause.)* It's an infinite sadness.

HE: What does sadness come doing here?

SHE: People often say 'an infinite sadness'. It's funny.

HE: *(Glum.)* Dead funny.

SHE: Yes. Just like your knife.

HE: I'll kill you one day.

SHE: You've been saying that for a long time.

HE: One day, I will.

SHE: *(Screaming.)* Now, that's not going to do anything anymore, does it? You should have done it before, before, a long time ago.

HE: Why before?

Someone knocks at the door.

MUSICIAN: Keep it quiet! Please!

SHE: Before, it could have avoided a lot of things. Now, it has no importance what so ever.

HE: It's true, it's too late. It can't change anything anymore now.

SHE: No. You can just close it and put it in your pocket.

HE: That would be a shame. Besides, I can't talk without a knife.

SHE: It's true. You always had it, your knife. For as long as I remember, you had that. And you always wanted to kill me. *(Pause.)* Has it already been of use, your knife?

HE: Of use? What do you mean?

SHE: I just wondered ... So, you've got it just for me?

HE: *(Tender.)* Yes, just for you.

SHE: That's sweet. That's very sweet. Put it on the table, so we can have a good look at it.

HE: Yes. Like this?

SHE: Yes, like that. It's beautiful.

HE: Yes, it's a beautiful knife. I like it a lot.

SHE: Me too. It's a shame it has never been of use.

HE: Yes, it's a shame. But that's how it is. *(Pause.)* They say it's never too late ...

SHE: Oh, they say lots of things ...

Scene Five

The children

HE and SHE drink. The sound of steps in the hallway. Several people pass. The laughter of women.

SHE: I have three children.

HE: You're joking.

SHE: They're not mine.

HE: So, you haven't got any.

SHE: I do. I have.

HE: I don't understand.

SHE: I have three children. I had them for someone else.

HE: What do you mean? Why?

SHE: I was asked to have them. Maybe their wives couldn't have any.

HE: What are they called?

SHE: Who?

HE: Your children?

SHE: I don't know. I don't even know if they were boys or girls. They immediately took them from me. They didn't show them to me.

HE: Where are they now?

SHE: I don't know. I never knew. They must be grown up by now.

HE: What did that do to you at the time?

SHE: It was very well paid.

HE: You never told me about that.

SHE: Why should I have told you about it?

HE: You're pulling my leg, aren't you?

SHE: Yes.

HE: And why three? It was triplets, was it?

SHE: No, they were born several years in between. They cried ... when they came out of me ... they took them away.

HE: Ha, ha! You had to dream all that!

SHE: Shut up!

HE: I'd still like to know ...

SHE: There's nothing to know. Go away!

HE: Your dreams ...

SHE: My dreams? You know, dreams, everyone has them, dreams.

HE: Well then, it's ... there's nothing else?

SHE: *(Screaming)* No! Nothing! Shoot!

HE: At what? With a knife?

The sound of footsteps behind the door. Someone knocks.

Scene Six

The Dream of Love

THE MUSICIAN: Shut-up! Shut-up! I can't take it anymore!

HE: How is he?

SHE: Who?

HE: Your musician.

SHE: As usual.

THE MUSICIAN: Open up! Let me in! *(HE rattles the door, then goes.)*

SHE: I'm tired. I don't know why I keep going. Out of habit, I suppose.

HE: No. To be able to see me.

SHE: To see you, I have my dreams.

HE: Your dreams? You're not angry anymore?

SHE: No. Give me your hand.

HE: Why?

SHE: It helps.

HE: I don't really like it.

HE sits on the floor next to the bed. HE takes her hand.

Short bit of music, false notes, then the noise of a violin crashed against the wall.

SHE: It's a street party … We walk the streets, you and me … I loved you. We walk together in a street celebrating.

HE: And then?

SHE: Then? *(Pause.)* I lost you in the crowd. I look for you. At the end of the street, there's a cafe. I go in. You are there. You are playing cards.

HE: I like playing cards.

SHE: You don't look at me, I leave. I don't like playing cards.

HE: We should have lived together.

SHE: Later, you hold me in your arms … People pass. You gesture to them not to wake me up. You protected my dreams …

HE: No way! I have better things to do during a party! *(HE gets up, pours himself a drink.)*

SHE: The ground is covered with dirty papers, broken bottles. It rains. The festive lights are off. It's the grey hour, before sunrise. A drunken man, like a nightmare, walks through the dead street. He walks in the rain, he cries, he shouts. Reeling with wine, anger, exhaustion, he lets himself drop on the doorstep of a house and with his sick forehead, he hits the heavy door, the door forever closed to a hopeless love. *(Pause.)* And he knocks, he knocks …

A gunshot, silence. HE, who amused had been listening to the woman, jumps.

HE: What was that?

SHE: Nothing. He flips every time. *(SHE takes a mirror from the night table, and looks at herself.)* I should go to the hairdresser tomorrow. It's terrible, this hair turning yellow.

HE: Usually, when getting older, hair turns grey. Not yellow.

SHE: It's the dye.

HE: You dye your hair?

SHE: What did you think? That I was blonde?

HE: I don't know. I never thought about it.

SHE: I completely forgot the colour of my hair, its real colour. Still … it was brown … When I was a young girl.

HE: You? You were a young girl?

Scene Seven

The Young Girl and the City

SHE: Yes, I was a young girl who walked in the street.

HE: You walked? Already?

SHE: I couldn't stay at home in the evening. I went out, I became prey.

HE: Don't exaggerate.

SHE: You're right. I walked in the street, simply that.

HE: Still now, you walk in the street.

SHE: Yes, I walk. But it's completely different. I'm not afraid of getting raped anymore.

HE: What are you afraid of?

SHE: What can I still be afraid of?

HE: Of the rape of your soul.

SHE: Of my soul? I don't even know what that is anymore.

HE: Your parents didn't say anything, about you walking in the street?

SHE: What makes you think I had parents?

HE: In general, people do. You didn't have any?

SHE: I did. But I could have been an orphan.

HE: You could have, yes. And your parents let you walk in the street in the evening?

SHE: They didn't know about it. They weren't there, they were asleep, they were drunk ... I had a lot of possibilities.

HE: I see. So you walked and you were afraid of being raped.

SHE: Not really. I wasn't really afraid.

HE: I see. And did they rape you?

SHE: Not really. And not in the street. In the street, I was alone.

HE: Alone? You liked that already?

SHE: Yes. I liked the road, the silence, the fear. I also liked knives. I already waited for you. It's there where I prefer to dream of you, there, in the street where I walked when I was a young girl. In another city, in another country. The street was wide, bordered with little white houses and immense chestnut trees. In the beginning of summer, these trees cried white tears, white petals that covered the ground with a layer so thick that I couldn't even hear the sound of my own steps. *(SHE closes her eyes.)* I walk there, alone, light as these petals. I'm in a white dress, my dark hair floating behind me. At the end of the road, you're waiting for me.

HE: *(Stabbing the knife in the table.)* No!

SHE: *(Opening her eyes.)* You don't want to?

HE: No! I wasn't there! I never went into that city, you made it up, it doesn't exist! When I knew you, you already had blonde hair. *(He drops his head between his arms, maybe he cries.)*

SHE: Don't be jealous.

SHE gets up, goes to the table, pours a drink, then strokes the head of the man. In the next room a violin is being tuned.

Scene Eight

Tantrums and Tender Feelings

HE: *(Shaking his head.)* I don't want to be loved!

SHE: *(Sits down on a chair in front of him.)* Don't worry. I haven't loved anyone yet.

HE: Not even me?

SHE: You? Grotesque! Why you? Have you seen yourself?

HE: Yes, I know … But then, your dreams?

SHE: What, my dreams? You pay me for that, no?

HE: I pay you to talk to me.

SHE: Yes, because my body doesn't interest you anymore. Not young enough anymore. When I was young, they bought my body. Now, they try to buy my dreams, my soul. You can't buy a soul.

HE: You haven't got one anymore.

SHE: Exactly. Well done.

HE: You are mean. I won't come back again. You disappoint me every time. When you were young, you already disappointed me with your body.

SHE: Look at that! And you, you think you were so brilliant in bed?

HE: I didn't have to be brilliant. I was paying. It was up to you to make an effort.

SHE: And it is still up to me to make an effort! To make up dreams!

HE: Obviously. I'm paying.

SHE: We are going to change roles now. Today, it's me who's paying. *(SHE takes the money from the table and throws it in his face. SHE grabs the knife.)*

And it's me who has the knife. Speak! Dream! Talk! Make something up!

HE: You're crazy!

SHE moves behind him, with one hand holds his arms, with the other puts the knife on his throat.

SHE: Why didn't you kill me, bastard? Why didn't you kill me twenty or thirty years ago? Why did you let me become old and ugly? Your money! As if I wanted your money! I've got a hundred times more than you, poor little pickpocket. It's your knife that I wanted, your beautiful shiny knife, in my breast, in my beautiful white breast when I was still young. It's your turn now. Go ahead, talk! Tell me your dreams!

HE: *(HE talks fast, HE is afraid.)* I never dream. But I always think of you. For thirty years, I've been thinking of you. If I didn't come more often, it was because I didn't have any money. I only came when I had money, a lot of money. To impress you ... The rest of the time, I was eating myself up with jealousy, thinking of the others, of all the others that marched through your legs. I suffered to bursting, but I never showed you. I knew I could never have you just to myself. If I'd managed a big hit ... then, maybe ... I hoped. I'm done hoping. I am done. If I still come to see you, it's not to make love anymore, it's ... not to be alone, always alone ... It's to be with you for a moment, to look at you, to listen to you ... And still now, you make me suffer. You torture me, you make me jealous with your lies, with your children, with your fake dreams. *(HE grabs the knife, HE straightens up.)* That was close! You got me scared, bitch!

SHE: *(SHE sits back on her bed, smiles.)* It was for a bit of a change. Admit it, this time you got your money's worth.

HE: This is the last time you see me! I am your last client. I bet you haven't got any left, hey? I'm the only one still coming.

SHE: Why would you be the only one? There are others that have known me for thirty years and continue to come and talk for an hour or two.

HE: *(Slumped on his chair.)* Even that ... her remains ... her decrepit body, her alcoholic chatter, her old age, yes, even her old age I have to share with others.

A hesitant music rises.

HE: Well. He's not dead?

SHE: Why would he be dead? Listen. What you said before, about the money ... You could have come even when you didn't have any. You could have come if you wanted to. I even would have given you some, money.

HE: Well! You would have made a pimp out of me! And she calls that love! Thanks, I have my dignity. I am a thief, but not a pimp. I always paid whores! *(HE returns the scattered money back on the table.)*

SHE: But now that you only come to talk, you really don't need to bring any money. You could come more often, every day ...

The music continues, more and more assured.

Scene Nine

The Provocation

HE: Everyday? Ah, yes? I could even come and live here, maybe?

SHE: No, not here.

HE: Not here, no. But with your savings you could buy a little house in a quiet street where nobody knows you. Yes?

SHE: Yes, I could …

HE: You could, couldn't you? And you wouldn't put anymore make-up on, you wouldn't dye your hair again? No?

SHE: No.

HE: Your grey hair, you would put it up in a beautiful bun and you'd wear a dress in a discreet colour? Yes?

SHE nods her head: 'Yes.'. SHE begins to doze off.

HE: And you wouldn't wear high heels anymore and you wouldn't have anymore red nails? No?

SHE shakes, no.

HE: And you'd cook, do the dishes, the washing, while I tend the roses in the garden? Yes?

SHE nods yes.

HE: And you wouldn't drink anymore alcohol, you wouldn't smoke anymore and you wouldn't go out walking alone in the street anymore? No?

SHE shakes, no.

HE: And we'd go to bed very early in the evening and, on Sunday afternoon, our grand children would come and visit us? Yes?

SHE nods, yes.

HE: What?! Yes?

SHE: Yes.

HE: You said 'yes'?

The music derails.

SHE: *(Jumping.)* What? Who? Ah, you're still here? *(SHE lays down turns her back on him.)*

HE: We could go to church from time to time, while we're at it.

HE looks at her, she doesn't respond anymore.

Scene Ten
The Farewell of the Thief

HE closes his knife, puts it in his pocket. HE gets up, walks to the bed. HE looks at her. SHE doesn't move. HE looks at her bag, hanging on a chair. HE looks at her again, then takes the bag. HE goes through it. HE takes out a bundle of notes, he counts them. SHE turns, looks at him, then turns towards the wall. HE puts the notes in his pocket. HE hesitates. HE takes out the bundle, takes a note, puts it next to the others on the table. HE lines them up, counts them, puts the rest back in his pocket. HE walks towards the door, takes his overcoat and his hat. HE turns the key, opens the door. HE comes back, switches the night lamp off. It's the grey hour, just before the sun rises. The pale dawn enters through the window.

HE: *(Looking outside, ironic.)* The dawn in all its splendour!

HE leaves banging the door. It stays open, balancing on its hinges.

Scene Eleven
The End of the Story

Music, free from the evils of the night, fills the room. THE MUSICIAN, playing the violin, enters. HE stops in the middle of the stage, his high and skinny silhouette shows against the window.

SHE pushes herself up on one elbow, looks at him.

HE puts his violin and bow on the table, pulls out a gun from his pocket, aims at the woman, shoots.

SHE falls on the bed.

Immediate curtains.

Neuchatel, 1984 (Original Version, 1975).

THE MONSTER

Characters

This play takes place in a fictional world inhabited by primitive people, almost naked, wearing masks. It consists of six scenes which can be played on a bare stage.

Scene One

The Arrival of the Monster

Night. The noise of chains and bells at the back of the stage. A horrible cry. A young man, NOB, moves up onto the stage. Low light.

NOB: *(Whispering.)* Tim. Tim. *(Louder.)* Tim. Wake up. *(He shakes TIM, who lays asleep on the floor. TIM wakes up.)* There is an enormous animal in the great pit, Tim. A weird animal.

TIM: You are a pretty weird animal yourself, Nob. It is really too early for me to get up.

NOB: No, Tim, really. I want you to come and have a look at it. You'll be so amazed. You have never seen an animal so big and so horrible.

TIM: A horrible animal? What kind of an animal, Nob? It must look like something, surely.

NOB: No. That's just it, Tim. I swear it resembles nothing, like nothing that we have seen before.

TIM: But that can wait till the morning, Nob. That can surely wait till morning.

NOB: No, Tim, I don't think so. I don't know what to do and … I'm afraid.

TIM: Afraid, Nob? You? Are you afraid?

NOB: Yes, I am afraid. So come, Tim. We will then decide together what would be the best thing to do. Aren't you my best friend, Tim? I need you.

TIM: That looks serious, Nob. Alright, I follow you. *(He gets up.)* But what do I hear? What's that weird sound?

NOB: That's the animal, Tim. It's the breathing of the animal that you hear.

TIM: That's impossible. From that far?

NOB: Yes, Tim. Isn't it disturbing?

TIM: Let's go and see.

They move down the back of the stage.

NOB: I don't want to. I'd rather not see it again. Go, Tim. Find out by yourself.

TIM: This is more and more strange.

He disappears in the night, then returns.

NOB: Have you seen it, Tim? You look pale.

TIM turns around, moves away a little. We can hear him vomit. He returns.

TIM: Wake up everyone. You, go get the Venerable One. He will decide upon what to do. I will take the drum.

NOB leaves. TIM takes his drum. He plays in the middle of the stage. MEN and WOMEN run up hastily from all sides. The MEN are armed. There are several outcries, tears from the women who sense the misfortune.

THE WOMEN: Misfortune, misfortune
Peace has ended
What danger threatens us
Misfortune, misfortune
What will happen
To our children
So gracious
So fragile
So innocent
Misfortune, misfortune
What will happen
To our men
So strong
So brave
So handsome
Misfortune, misfortune
A great danger threatens us

NOB arrives with the VENERABLE ONE, a bony old man, which induces a silence. The VENERABLE ONE places himself in the centre of the group of people, facing the audience.

VENERABLE ONE: *(To NOB.)* Speak!

NOB: I was on guard duty tonight, by the great pit. I was asleep.

VENERABLE ONE: That is allowed.

NOB: The noise of chains and bells woke me. I went to have a look. It is … It is an animal that we have never seen around here. It's enormous, it resembles nothing, and it expels a pungent smell.

TIM: An unbearable smell. It made me feel sick.

VENERABLE ONE: Is it dead?

NOB: No. It is breathing. You can hear it from here.

VENERABLE ONE: Let us listen!

Silence. The panting of the Monster can be heard.

VENERABLE ONE: Alive! Despite the poisoned thorns at the bottom of the pit! Women, return to your homes. Men, follow me!

The WOMEN disperse. The MEN leave, singing and dancing, towards the back of the stage.

MEN: We are the men
Who are very brave
We will defend our women
Our children
Our houses
Against all danger
Against all threat
Nothing scares us
We will be victorious
We are the men

The back lights up. The sun rises. The MEN surround the pit with upfront the VENERABLE ONE.

MEN: It is so ugly
It stinks
It's slimy
Disgusting
Monstrous
Dreadful

VENERABLE ONE: Lift your spears!

The MEN lift their spears and after a shout from the VENERABLE ONE, they strike into the flesh of the Monster. Silence. The Monster keeps breathing.)

VENERABLE ONE: Retract your spears!

The MEN retract their spears and examine the points.

MEN: No blood! No blood! No blood!

Drum. Silence.

VENERABLE ONE: Your bows. Your poisoned arrows!

The MEN, after a sign from the VENERABLE ONE, send their arrows into the back of the Monster. The breathing continues.

VENERABLE ONE: Stones!

The MEN collect big stones, running all around. They lift them together and, after a shout from the VENERABLE ONE, hurl them towards the MONSTER. The breathing continues.

VENERABLE ONE: Let us pray!

ALL: Sole God of our sole world
Eternal God of our eternal world
Come to our aid
We have become weak and vulnerable
We bow down into the dust
Wake your children
Our sorrow is great
Oh! We are in need of you
Sole God of our sole world
Eternal God of our eternal world

Scene Two

NOB and LIL

NOB enters with a guitar. Singing, or rather, trying to sing.

NOB: The shadow
falls
on the river

the dew on the fields
listen to the silence
the steps of the wind
that is coming closer
talking to us
touching us

He stops, discouraged. Sits down. Enter LIL, a YOUNG GIRL.

LIL: Go on, Nob. Sing. It's so beautiful.

NOB: No, Lil. It's not beautiful. It doesn't work anymore. Look, I can't tune my guitar. And look at my fingers. I have a cramp in my fingers each time I try to play. My voice is hoarse and I am becoming tired. Look at the shadows. They have never been so dark. I am trembling, Lil! I am trembling and I am scared. Ever since the Monster has been amongst us, I have been restless and sad.

LIL: What monster are you talking about, Nob?

NOB: What monster? That disgusting animal we found one night in the great pit and that we didn't manage to kill. How it disgusted everyone. It was smelly and slimy. All who laid eyes on it fell ill. But then, they became used to it. And then ... they started to like it. I don't understand. I can't understand, how could that have happened?

LIL: You don't understand, Nob? Go and see. That what you call a monster doesn't exist anymore. Its grey and rugged back is covered with magnificent flowers, and these flowers give off delicious perfumes.

NOB: Perfumes! It stinks, despite everything, it stinks up to here. You can smell its nauseating stink everywhere. It penetrates the houses, the woods, going as deep as the bottom of the lake. We're all soaked with it. Our hair, our clothes, our food, you smell it everywhere.

LIL: What an idea! It doesn't smell, even when you get very close to it... It doesn't smell of anything but the scent of flowers.

NOB: Oh, you don't smell it? And his heavy breathing, heaving, you don't hear that either? You cannot escape that obsessive noise, obscene, sickening. I can even hear

it when I play, even when I sing, even when I sleep. It
disturbs my sleep, I hear it in my dreams.

LIL: You are exaggerating, Nob. It's true, you can hear it,
but it's not that bad. Quite the opposite, it has something
reassuring and agreeable about it. We would miss that
sound if it suddenly stopped. You see, Nob. You were
always too sensitive. And you have become too much of a
loner. You never come with us, to sing and dance around
it. You wander, alone and sad over the rocks with your
guitar. Your eyes become more and more sombre and
you keep them fixed further and further away. You have
changed a lot, Nob.

NOB: Everything has changed here. The air, the people,
everything, all of life. I am afraid, Lil. I feel as if a great
danger looms over us.

LIL: *(Laughing.)* What danger? It's the opposite, life is
becoming more and more beautiful.

NOB: The Monster is becoming bigger, Lil. It grows constantly,
you know it very well.

LIL: So what? It grows. There is enough space.

NOB: Space, maybe, there is still enough, yes. But the Monster
eats more and more, it feels stronger and stronger and it
breaths louder and louder. And … it eats everything, even
men.

LIL: Oh, you are so irritating! It didn't do it on purpose. It was
… it was nothing else but careless people who happened to
be just before his mouth. It closed his mouth, that's all. It
definitely isn't mean. It can't even move around.

NOB: Every now and then it crushes a child under his feet …

LIL: It is heavy and clumsy, that's all. It doesn't do it out of
menace. Mothers should watch their children a bit better.

NOB: It's strange how everyone defends it, even you.

LIL: Yes, I defend it, because I love it. Everyone loves it,
except you. Because you have never inhaled the scent of its
amazing flowers.

NOB: I've heard talk about that. They say that when they breathe the scent of its flowers, these flowers that have grown on his hideous back, yes, it seems, by smelling these flowers, they feel a strange wellbeing, an unknown happiness.

LIL: Yes, Nob, and all fear disappears, and all the anguish and all the sadness. Even the physical pains. The elderly forget that they are old, and the sick forget their illnesses. It cures all that is bad, it cures the soul.

NOB: For a moment, maybe, for a certain time. But the Monster grows, Lil, don't forget that it grows very quickly. It has already taken the place of our old village. We had to rebuild our houses somewhere else, replant our gardens further up. And, in a few months, we'll have to start again.

LIL: Surely one day it will stop growing, no?

NOB: How do you know that?

LIL: But … It can't be any different.

NOB: Why not?

LIL: Because … Because … There won't be no more place … for us.

Silence.

LIL: You scare me, Nob. You see everything so dark. You'll see, everything will work out fine.

NOB: I don't think so, Lil, sadly enough. I don't believe it.

LIL: Let's try and get some sleep, will you?

NOB: Lil, I want to see your soul.

LIL: Oh, Nob! We shouldn't unveil our soul except before the man we marry or before death.

NOB: You also can before the man you love.

LIL: I love you, Nob.

LIL takes her mask off. NOB takes his off. They look at each other.

NOB: Now we are as husband and wife.

LIL: But what sadness in your soul, poor Nob. Tomorrow, you will come with me. The Monster, as you call it, will heal you.

NOB: It is you who needs healing, Lil. You and all the others.

LIL: Let us sleep now, it is late.

They fall asleep in each other's arms.

Scene Three

The dream

Masked men, carrying a coffin, enter. The man who walks upfront plays the trumpet. The procession circles NOB and LIL then stops in front of the couple.

NOB: Who are you burying?

FIRST MAN: Nobody.

SECOND MAN: It is not a burial. It's a birth.

They place the coffin on the ground and lift the cover.

ALL: These are the offspring of the Monster. The Monster has given birth tonight. See here the magnificent babies of the Monster.

Out of the coffin they lift small monsters, in the shape of repulsive animals, wrapped in rags. They toss them in the air, shouting and full of joy. LIL catches one, clasps it in her arms and rocks it like a baby.

LIL: My beautiful baby, my small child. My sweet little monster! How beautiful you are, how cute you are! It's hungry, the poor little baby, It wants to feed, the poor little sweet.

She uncovers a breast and suckles the baby.

NOB: Lil! No, Lil! What are you doing?

LIL: Look it's adorable. It eats. Eat, little sweet, eat my little baby.

THIRD MAN: Catch!

*The THIRD MAN throws a monster to NOB, but NOB, disgusted, takes a
step back and the bundle of cloth crashes to the ground. This infuriates
the MEN. They attack NOB, who starts running around the stage.*

FIRST: You let it fall?

SECOND MAN: You don't want it?

SECOND MAN: You don't like them?

ALL: To death! To death!

*They catch NOB and tie him up with a rope. They put him in the
coffin and throw the monsters on top of him.*

FIRST MAN: There, something good for the little ones.

SECOND MAN: It's your favourite food.

THIRD MAN: Treat yourself, it's fresh.

LIL: Go, you too, my little one. Eat my little glutton.

*She throws her baby monster on NOB who is fighting and screaming.
All dance around the coffin. NOB pulls himself up and shakes the
monsters off. He has the beak of a bird and wings. He isn't tied up
anymore. He gets out of the coffin and takes his guitar. The others
look at him in silence. NOB walks away, playing his guitar.*

LIL: Where are you going, Nob?

NOB: Somewhere else.

LIL: There is nowhere else.

NOB: To another world.

LIL: There is no other world.

NOB: There is. For me. For me alone, there is one. A world
without shadows, a world without monsters.

LIL: Nob, don't go that way. You will fall, Nob, the abyss.

NOB: Don't you see? I am a bird. I have wings.

LIL: No-o-o-o-b!

*Night. Then a faint light. The coffin and the men have disappeared.
NOB and LIL lay asleep as before. It's dawn.*

LIL: Nob!

NOB: What's wrong? Why are you shouting, Lil?

LIL: You were holding me too tight. You almost choked me.

NOB: I was dreaming, Lil. I dreamed that ...

LIL: What did you dream, Nob?

NOB: I dreamed that I was a bird and that I flew up very high and very far away.

LIL: Without me, Nob?

NOB: Yes, without you. Alone.

Scene Four

The Alliance

The VENERABLE ONE sits on a reed mat. NOB arrives, stops at a distance.

NOB: I would like to talk to you, Venerable one.

VENERABLE ONE: Come closer, my son. Speak.

NOB: *(Approaching.)* Some time ago, I had a dream, father, a dream I can't seem to forget.

VENERABLE ONE: Tell it to me, my son.

NOB: First it was a nightmare. There were monsters, little monsters that were born from that horrible animal with the flowers on its back. Men put me in a coffin and they threw the monsters at me, so they could feed on my body. But I freed myself. I had become a large bird. I had wings and I flew away to another world.

VENERABLE ONE: There is no other world, son.

NOB: The world ... after death?

VENERABLE ONE: Death?

NOB: Death, and then another world?

(Silence.)

NOB: Why don't you answer me, Venerable One?

VENERABLE ONE: What do you expect from me?

NOB: I would like to leave. Like in my dream. To that world that awaits our souls after life. To that world you have spoken of so often…

VENERABLE ONE: Why? Why do you want to go? Why do you want to die, my son?

NOB: Because of the monster. I hate it. I hate it as much as I did on the first day.

VENERABLE ONE: Everyone seems to love it.

NOB: You too, father?

VENERABLE ONE: No, not me. I don't like it. I know it will cause our downfall, it will destroy us.

NOB: Then why don't you act, why don't you do something?

VENERABLE ONE: Do what, my son? We tried everything in the beginning. And now they are all for him. I am alone and old.

NOB: No, you are not alone. I am with you.

VENERABLE ONE: You want to leave…

NOB: I don't want to keep living here. I want to live in the world that follows after death. That world you have told us of so often. That world, father, does it exist?

Silence.

NOB: Answer me, father. I have to know. I have the right to know.

VENERABLE ONE: Yes, you have the right to know. That world exists, my son, but, I fear, in that world, there is nothing but darkness.

Silence.

NOB: So, my dream … What does it mean, my dream?

VENERABLE ONE: Your dream means that you will find that world of light. You will find it not after death, but here, in our world. Your dream means that you will defeat the monster.

NOB: Me? Why me?

VENERABLE ONE: Tell me, my son, have you already inhaled the perfume of these fantastic flowers?

NOB: Never, father.

VENERABLE ONE: That there, is your strength. You are the only one together with me, who has not done so.

NOB: And I never will, because I know it will be the end of me, that I will start loving it as the others do, and I will be defeated.

VENERABLE ONE: It is you who will be the victor, my son, I am sure of that. You fill my soul with hope. I don't feel alone anymore. With your courage and my wisdom, we will be stronger than the Monster.

NOB: But what can we do against him?

VENERABLE ONE: Go home in peace, my son. I will think. When the hour comes, I will call you.

NOB: I will impatiently wait for your call. You have given me my courage back. You have given me my life back.

NOB goes on his way, playing his guitar, singing.

NOB: In my eyes are reflecting
The colours of the sky
Through my hair there play
The fingers of a breeze
Again in my heart
Joy and peace are born
The churning of my soul
Is giving way to hope
The earth will be returned
To the people of our world
There they will grow
Pure and beautiful flowers

Scene Five

The Decision

The VENERABLE ONE sits on his mat, surrounded by young men, amongst those NOB and TIM.

VENERABLE ONE: I have chosen you for your youth and your courage. I have taken an important decision. Before telling you about it, I want to know if I can count on you without restriction.

ALL: Yes, Venerable One.

VENERABLE ONE: Well then. I allow you to sit down, because this will take long. You all know, the Monster grows at a frightening speed. Once again we must rebuild our houses elsewhere and replant our gardens, because it has taken the space of our second village. This cannot go on like this. If the Monster doesn't stop growing, we don't know where to go anymore. We will have no more space to live.

ALL: No more space ... to live!

VENERABLE ONE: So we have to act and stop the Monster from growing.

ALL: Stop it from growing!

VENERABLE ONE: Through observation and through reflection, I have come to the only possible solution.

ALL: He has found it!

VENERABLE ONE: The only way to stop the Monster from growing is to deprive it from its favourite food, which is human flesh.

ALL: Human flesh!

VENERABLE ONE: Yes, I observed that after devouring a human being, that found itself before his mouth, the Monster immediately grew in an unbelievable way. While on the other hand, when it had only its usual feed for a certain time, not only did it keep its normal size, it shrunk visibly. My conclusion is the following: if we deprive the Monster of human flesh and of all other feed for a time span long enough, its size will diminish more and more, up until its complete extinction.

ALL: Complete extinction!

VENERABLE ONE: For that, we have to stop people from approaching it. I know that will not please everyone. They have grown used to the Monster, they need it. They like to inhale the poison of the flowers.

A MAN: The poison?

VENERABLE ONE: Yes, it's a poison that numbs their spirit, that gives them a sense of wellbeing.

A MAN: An immense wellbeing!

VENERABLE ONE: An illusion of wellbeing that cannot last. Even amongst you, there are certainly some who would not do without it anymore.

ALL: Do without it? Forever?

VENERABLE ONE: Yes, forever. We have to make a choice. Death for all, or the extinction of the Monster.

ALL: Not death! Not death!

VENERABLE ONE: Those in favour of the Monster can leave. They can again approach it, inhale the venom of its flowers, until they are so dizzy, they fall before its open mouth. Feed it with your bodies! Let it swell up more and more!

NOB: So you think, Venerable One, that it is the perfume of the flowers that makes people fall numb before his open mouth?

VENERABLE ONE: Without a doubt. It's a trick from the Monster, who cannot move, cannot move around. It is in this way that he gets hold of his favourite food, the only food that really suits him.

NOB: Do you hear that? Do you understand? It's your body it wants. That immense wellbeing he gives you, is to lure you into his hideous mouth.

VENERABLE ONE: We have to choose. That those who want to leave, leave.

Nobody moves.

VENERABLE ONE: You all stayed. Thank you. I will reveal to you my plans. The time is right. We have to act fast. People again have to rebuild their houses elsewhere. They are not in favour of the Monster. They start to be afraid. The first thing to do is to build a wall of stone around the Monster. That the whole population take part in this. Tell them it is to prevent the Monster from growing. They will agree. The second thing: gather all weapons and throw them in the abyss.

ALL: Disarm the men?

VENERABLE ONE: Yes, by force or by deception. Disarm them all. Except for you. You keep your weapons, because you will need them. *(Pause.)* You will need them, because in the future you will shoot whoever approaches the wall that we will have build around the Monster. Shoot without pity, without consideration. At your parents, at your friends, without distinction.

ALL: Without distinction!

VENERABLE ONE: Even between yourselves, those that fail, those that want to go over the wall … the others have to kill them without hesitation.

ALL: Without hesitation!

VENERABLE ONE: It is cruel, I know. But otherwise we all are doomed. Do you understand me?

ALL: Yes, Venerable One.

VENERABLE ONE: Are you ready to complete this bloody task in order to save our world?

ALL: We are ready.

(Singing.)

We will kill
We will kill
Without weakness
Without pity
We will kill
To save our world

We will kill people
So that others may live
So the monster dies
Without weakness
Without pity
We will kill.

Scene Six

The disappearance of the Monster

The VENERABLE ONE sits on his mat, alone. In the back of the stage, NOB stands guard. He is alone. The sound of footsteps. A MAN arrives.

NOB: Stop there, man! Don't go there!

MAN: Have pity.

NOB: On who?

MAN: On me.

NOB: I don't know you. I already killed my parents. The young girl that I loved, Lil, I also killed her. I have killed my best friend, Tim. I have killed children. Why should I have pity on you?

MAN: I know. You are merciless. You've also killed your fellow guards.

NOB: They failed. They wanted to approach the Monster. I killed them. All of them. So the Monster would disappear. And I succeeded. In a few days there will be nothing left of him.

MAN: And what good would that do? In the village either, there is no one left.

NOB: What did you say?

MAN: I am the last inhabitant of the village. You and your mates have killed everyone.

NOB: Everyone?

MAN: The Venerable One is left … and you … and me. But I don't want to live anymore. What good is it to live in solitude, without wellbeing?

NOB: Wellbeing?

MAN: You, you have never known it. The wellbeing that comes from the perfume of the flowers …

NOB: No, I have never known it.

MAN: That's why you have no pity. You only know hate. You are filled with hate.

NOB: Without hate, I could not have done what I did. I needed to have that hate for him, in order to defeat him.

MAN: You have become a monster yourself. You have done nothing but killing for months. You have exterminated your people.

NOB: I have saved our world.

MAN: You have saved it for yourself alone. It's yours now, the world! And what are you going to do with it?

NOB: You are still alive, you too. Leave, or I will kill you.

MAN: I am not asking you to let me live, because I came here to die. I have lost all those I loved. I want to join them in death. But let me die close to the Monster. Let me inhale one more time the perfume of its flowers. Let me feel that wellbeing one last time.

NOB: And the Monster will eat you and grow again. And we would have to wait again for weeks or months for it to disappear. While its extinction is now so close.

MAN: What does that matter now? A few more weeks, a few more months? How can that change anything? For who? For what?

NOB: For me. I want my job to be done. That the Monster be gone. I have enough. I killed too much. I have waited too long. Stop, I am telling you. Don't come closer. Do not approach the wall. I will shoot!

He bends his bow, shoots. A scream. The man falls. NOB throws his bow away, climbs the wall and looks. He jumps of the wall and runs to the VENERABLE ONE.

NOB: I've won! I've won! The Monster is no more!

VENERABLE ONE: Come closer, Nob. I am going to die.

NOB: It's over, father.

VENERABLE ONE: Yes, it's over. Your dream has become reality, Nob. You will live in a world without a monster. Alone. Then you will die, alone. Alone, Nob, are you listening? *(Pause.)* The Monster has won, Nob. It has killed us. It has killed … life. I was wrong, maybe. Should I have let the people die in the illusive wellbeing of the flowers? Maybe, I don't know anymore. It's too late. I was wrong yes, but it's too late.

The VENERABLE ONE takes his mask off, puts it next to him, lays down, moves no more.

NOB: I defeated the Monster! I won! It's me who has won!

He looks around him, sees TIM's drum on the ground, takes it. He walks around the stage, playing the drum.

NOB: Come, come all! I won, I defeated the Monster! We will live again in joy, in peace. Come all! We will have a big feast. Come my friends, young and old! We will sing, we will dance. Lil, where are you? Come dance, Lil! Tim, where are you? Come sing with me! Come all! Come!

NOB drops the drum, stops, looks around him, lost. He returns to the old man.

NOB: But, where are they all? Where have they gone? *(He shakes his head.)* I don't understand. Where are Lil, Tim and the others? I don't understand. *(Pause.)* Here's my guitar. *(He takes his guitar from the ground, it has no more strings. For a long time he stares at it.)* Here's my guitar.

NOB pushes the old man over and takes his place on the reed mat, in the same position as the VENERABLE ONE. He changes his mask with that of the VENERABLE ONE.

NOB: *(With an old man's voice.)* This happened here or
elsewhere
Somewhere
One day
Today, yesterday or tomorrow

THE ROAD

Characters

THE SUIT

THE SINGER

THE GARDENER

THE MOTHER

THE BABY

THE PAINTER

THE DANCER

THE SCHOLAR

THE SAD WOMAN

THE HAPPY WOMAN

THE GAINSAYER

THE GIRL

THE YOUNG MAN

THE OLD WOMAN

THE MAD MAN

OFF STAGE VOICE

MURMURS

Imagine a time, far in the future.

The ground is completely covered with concrete. There are only roads left. There is nothing else. The people, born on the road, live on the road. On foot they walk these roads that were constructed for the traffic of cars. The cars stopped working a long time ago. They are but abandoned carcassses. They call them the 'shelters'. Mankind has fallen back into a primitive state and knows our civilisation only through 'legends'.

These 'legends' talk of the sun, stars, earth, mud, flowers, grass, trees, houses.

Superstition or truth? Some believe in them. Others think the Earth, from the beginning of time, was covered with concrete and fog.

The questions are: Where do the roads lead? Do they have an end? Why directions? Why the walk? Do the exits exist? Are they real or false?

But rest assured. For the moment this is but a nightmare. The nightmare of a 'road engineer'.

SCENE ONE

A motorway. Everything is colourless and dull. Crossings, junctions, tunnels, faded road signs, broken cars, abandoned. Shadows move around. A man in a suit enters from right, he walks, carrying an empty can.

MURMURS: He ran out … he ran out … he ran out …

OFF STAGE VOICE: He ran out of fuel.

> *To the left, two road signs light up. One says: 'All directions.' The other: 'Other directions.'*

THE SUIT: It's stupid. Extremely stupid. What to do?

> *Distraught, he stops, drops his can, sits on the side of the road.*

MURMURS: Walk … walk … never stop. It's dangerous to stop … it's dangerous to sit down … walk … walk …

OFF STAGE VOICE: It is strictly forbidden to park by the side of the road without the sidelights on.

THE SUIT: I can't go on anymore. I'll wait here. A car has to pass by one day.

OFF STAGE VOICE: A car? What is that?

THE SUIT: My head! Too much champagne. Hung-over. Who cares! My project has been approved! And what a project! Bridges, tunnels, crossings, junctions, viaducts, exits, entries, straight lines, curved lines. The whole thing could not be more complicated and more expensive. A marvel!

SCENE TWO

A woman enters dressed in very colourful rags. She speaks in a singing voice.

THE SINGER: So young, so young, and already tired? So young, so young, and already nearly dead?

THE SUIT: *(Stands up.)* Madame! You too? Broken down? Or worse? An accident?

THE SINGER: Your're not dying then? I'm quite hungry, though. That's a shame. Goodbye. I carry on my way.

THE SUIT: But, Madame, stop. Where are you going?

THE SINGER: Where the road leads me. Straight ahead, always onward.

THE SUIT: Rather wait here, with me.

THE SINGER: Wait? Why wait?

THE SUIT: You could walk for hours and hours on this road without finding a gas pump, or a help post, or a motel, or an exit.

THE SINGER: Ah, you're looking for an exit. There are quite a few people looking for them. Not me. What I do is sing. That will do me. *(In a spoken voice.)* If you want to know, exits don't exist. Even there where there are signs saying 'Exit', it's a bluff. They're false exits. They lead nowhere. They simply lead to other roads.

THE SUIT: *(Aside.)* Poor woman. *(To The Singer.)* Help will come. Wait here with me.

THE SINGER: *(In a singing voice.)* With you? Why with you? I always sing alone. I am a soloist. I don't need anyone. I don't know you.

THE SUIT: But you do. We were introduced yesterday evening, at the reception, at the Mayor's house.

THE SINGER: What do you sing me there?

THE SUIT: Yes, at the reception given in my honour. It was me who won the competition of the new south-west highway project, cutting in two the eastern area of the northern hemisphere.

THE SINGER: What lines! I would love to sing them. But they are a little bit complicated for me, I am afraid. Goodbye, Sir! Do not torment yourself. All this is but a funny dream.

(She exits.)

OFF STAGE VOICE: A dream that seems to turn into a nightmare.

THE SUIT: And to say that she is the most famous singer of our times! She was, maybe. But then, yesterday evening … She definitely had an accident, a concussion, a shock. She's completely mad. *(He sits down again.)* My feet hurt. *(He takes his shoes off and massages his feet.)* I am cold. What a mist! And not a breeze. It's unbelievable! For hours, not a single car. In fact, what time is it? *(He looks at his watch.)* May 28, 23 hours 59 minutes. But that was yesterday! My watch has stopped.

SCENE THREE

THE SUIT is on stage. Another man enters. He wants to walk straight on, but THE SUIT stops him.

THE SUIT: Another pedestrian. Bizarre. Sir! I think I know you. We have already met somewhere.

THE GARDENER: On the road everything is possible, but not very probable, and never certain.

THE SUIT: I've got it. You're the Mayor's gardener. I saw you yesterday evening in the Mayor's winter garden. Let me introduce myself: Edmond Dubéton. Bridge and road engineer. It's my project that won the prize. I've been given the commission.

THE GARDENER: Well, gosh. So much chatter. I don't like talking. It tires me.

THE SUIT: What are you doing here, on the road?

THE GARDENER: I walk. What else could I do?

THE SUIT: But why are you on the road?

THE GARDENER: Where else could I be?

THE SUIT: In your bed. In your garden?

THE GARDENER: I don't know what that is.

THE SUIT: You don't know what what is?

THE GARDENER: What you say. Beh, dargen.

THE SUIT: Garden. You don't know what a garden is?

THE GARDENER: No. I don't know a lot of words. I talk little. It doesn't interest me.

THE SUIT: That's extraordinary. Complete amnesia. He also suffered a shock. Maybe they were in the same car. That must be it: it was him driving The Singer's car. What shall I do? Let's try word association. Listen, my good man. I will tell you a word and you reply with another word, any word, the first that comes to mind. Agreed?

THE GARDENER: If it amuses you …

THE SUIT: *(Staring in his eyes.)* Tree.

THE GARDENER: Road.

THE SUIT: Bushes.

THE GARDENER: Road.

THE SUIT: Grass.

THE GARDENER: Road.

THE SUIT: Another word. Not always the same one. Change your answers. Flowers.

THE GARDENER: Concrete.

THE SUIT: Birds.

THE GARDENER: Concrete.

THE SUIT: Butterfly.

GARDENER: Con …

THE SUIT: No! Not always concrete! You must remember some other words aside from road and concrete!

THE GARDENER: Well, not really.

THE SUIT: Let's try once more. Vegetables.

THE GARDENER: Meat.

THE SUIT: We're there! You said: meat. The word vegetable reminded you of the word meat. You can eat both things.

THE GARDENER: Well, I happen to be hungry.

THE SUIT: You would happily eat a big plate of beans …

THE GARDENER: I don't know what that is, 'peams'. But I know what you are. An inventor of words. I have already met people like you. They have fun with saying words nobody understands. And they are proud of that, and they call themselves intellectis, or something like that. And instead of walking, they stop to talk and waste their time. I haven't got time to waste, I have to walk, and find something to eat. I am a simple man, me, I am a normal man. *(While leaving.)* I am starving. He sure has tired me out with his stupid questions. That'll teach me. *(He exits.)*

SCENE FOUR

A YOUNG GIRL enters from right, dancing.

THE SUIT: The Mayor's daughter! Last night, I danced with her and I decided to marry her. I owe that to my career, to my genius. I will marry her, yes. Half of the road has already been laid, that is, I agree. All there's missing is her consent. Miss!

The dancer doesn't reply, she dances around THE SUIT in a rather seductive way.

THE SUIT: So beautiful you are! How well you dance!

She brushes against him while dancing.

THE SUIT: Oh my, you would say she likes me. But then, last night I didn't please her at all.

129

She takes him by the arm.

THE SUIT: I don't know how to dance that well.

He clumsily tries. She guides him, pulls him towards a 'shelter', she is pointing out with her finger. The shelter is the skeleton of a car with a sign 'SHELTER' that lights up.

THE SUIT: In there? But it's an old skeleton of a car. You want that ... you and me ... before marriage? In an abandoned car? Well now, Miss! What would your father say?

The DANCER pushes him forcefully and impatiently towards the 'shelter'.

THE SUIT: I can't resist such charm.

THE DANCER: You talk too much, instead of doing something.

Both of them exit.

SCENE FIVE

A SAD WOMAN enters, soon followed by a HAPPY WOMAN.

THE SAD WOMAN: This road, always the same. This fog, always the same. Oh, to see the sun once! Just for once!

THE HAPPY WOMAN: *(With a big smile.)* What's that, the sun?

THE SAD WOMAN: I won't tell you. You make fun of me. You laugh at me.

THE HAPPY WOMAN: I am not making fun of you. I laugh because I am happy, that's all. I am always happy.

THE SAD WOMAN: I am always sad. It's because of the fog ... Everything is grey, everything is sad, because there is never any sun.

THE HAPPY WOMAN: What is it, the sun?

THE SAD WOMAN: The sun is warmth, light, colours.

THE HAPPY WOMAN: That must be beautiful and cheerful.

THE SAD WOMAN: Yes. If you like, I'll tell you everything. Everything an old woman told me one day. She was told this by another and another, even older.

THE HAPPY WOMAN: What did they say?

THE SAD WOMAN: It was a very, very long time ago, very far away in time ... at that time, they walked on the ground, or on grass ...

THE HAPPY WOMAN: What's that?

THE SAD WOMAN: I don't know. It was soft, it didn't hurt your feet.

THE HAPPY WOMAN: That must have been fun. They didn't walk on concrete then?

THE SAD WOMAN: No, there was no concrete, and there was no road.

THE HAPPY WOMAN: No road? That's too weird! Then where were the people?

THE SAD WOMAN: In houses. Houses were like shelters, but much bigger. You could stay in there for a very long time.

THE HAPPY WOMAN: Why stay? Did people not walk all the time?

THE SAD WOMAN: Very little. They didn't need to walk.

OFF STAGE VOICE: They drove by car.

THE HAPPY WOMAN: But if they didn't walk, what did they do? Did they have fun?

THE SAD WOMAN: They looked at the sun, the clouds, the moon, the stars.

OFF STAGE VOICE: And mostly television. In colour.

THE HAPPY WOMAN: Where were those things?

THE SAD WOMAN: Up there, above all that greyness.

THE HAPPY WOMAN: Do you think they are still there? That would be wonderful!

THE SAD WOMAN: Yes, I believe so. It's just that we can't see them anymore.

THE HAPPY WOMAN: I am so happy to know there are lots of pretty things above us! But what you say about the roads, I don't believe that.

THE SAD WOMAN: Yet, there was a time when there weren't any roads.

THE HAPPY WOMAN: I was born on the road. You were born on the road. The road exists since the beginning of time. Everyone knows that. Your stories are just legends. But that doesn't matter. It's beautiful, it's amusing, I'm happier than before..

THE SAD WOMAN: How can you be happy on the road, where everything is monotonous, sadness, despair.

THE HAPPY WOMAN: Oh no! The road is life, movement, the walk, the road is adventure, love, friendship, the people you meet there. The stories you hear there. Come with me. We'll walk together.

THE SAD WOMAN: No, you walk too fast, and your laughter hurts me.

THE HAPPY WOMAN: Goodbye then. Don't be sad. The road holds some pleasant surprises for everyone.

She leaves.

THE SAD WOMAN: She didn't believe me, she as well, nobody believes me. *(While leaving.)* Just once, see the stars.

SCENE SIX

An OLD WOMAN arrives, painfully dragging a leg.

OLD WOMAN: I have to ... I have to keep going ... Walking ... Walking ... Don't lie down ... Don't die ... Not yet ... Not yet ...So tired. My legs are so heavy. My legs can't go on anymore. I have to rest a little. *(She looks around her.)* There's no one. *(She sits down.)* I'll gather some strength, and then ... then ... I will continue ... I will walk ... *(She lies down.)* Finally, finally. It's so nice to lie down.

NO1 arrives, comes closer, stops, touches the OLD WOMAN who jumps and sits back up again.

OLD WOMAN: Oh, it's just a little ... pain in the left foot. Nothing major, nothing serious, I'm resting, that's all. *(No1 sits down a few steps away from her.)* You can keep going. I don't need any help. *(Pause.)* What are you waiting for?

NO 2 arrives, looks at the OLD WOMAN, looks at NO1. Winking. Signs of understanding. NO2 sits down.)

OLD WOMAN: You too? I just said that I was holding up just fine. My left foot hurts a bit. That's all.

NO1 and NO2 slowly approach the OLD WOMAN. NO3 arrives, passes the group and sits down at the other side. NO4 the same thing. As NO5. The characters show their hunger. Some are getting impatient, lick their lips, swallow, drool. The OLD WOMAN is dying, but each time someone comes too close, she moves a leg or shakes her head to show that she is not dead. She can even snub them.)

OFF STAGE VOICE: Around the dying woman, awaiting the legacy, the relatives gallantly chatted, badly hiding their impatience.

No1: She could hurry up a bit.

No2: She could think about the others.

No3: What an egoist!

No4: Really, she's going too far.

No5: They're all like that.

The OLD WOMAN gets up with a great effort and stays up, unsteady. The others are stunned and furious.

No1: Shit!

No2: That's impossible.

No3: *(To THE OLD WOMAN.)* Don't insist. Let yourself go. Take a rest.

No4: Lie down gently. Would you like us to help you?

No5: Patience has its limits.

One of the characters grabs a sign post and from behind hits the OLD WOMAN on the head, who drops. The others jump on the OLD WOMAN. Night. A sign lights up: 'CROSSED FORK AND KNIFE.'

SCENE SEVEN

Enter a young boy dressed in a way to resemble as much as possible a big baby. He sucks his thumb. On hearing steps he turns around with a big smile.

THE BABY: Mammy!

Enter a ripe and sumptuous woman.

THE MOTHER: What, mammy? I am not your mother.

THE BABY: No, but you could be. I need a mammy.

THE MOTHER: Hold on! You've grown up now. You can manage very well on your own.

THE BABY: *(Jumping on the neck of the woman, holding on.)* I don't want to be big. I want to be carried and I want to be given milk. *(He fumbles inside the woman's blouse.)*

THE MOTHER: *(Pushing him off, sitting him on the ground.)* You should be ashamed!

THE BABY: I am not ashamed. I want a mammy.

THE MOTHER: You know all too well that from the moment a child can walk alone, it leaves its mother and takes another road. It's the law.

THE BABY: The law is stupid.

THE MOTHER: It's you who's stupid.

THE BABY: *(Whining.)* You never had children, you?

THE MOTHER: I did, I had several. They've grown up. They left.

THE BABY: I don't want to grow up. I don't want to leave.

THE MOTHER: You can't stay a baby forever.

THE BABY: Yes I can, if I want to. And I want to. I hold on to all the necks of all the women I meet. Sometimes they still have milk. I like milk.

THE MOTHER: You really are very stupid.

SCENE EIGHT

Enter a man, dragging along books, tied behind him. The MOTHER and the BABY are still there.

THE SCHOLAR: Yes, let's talk about stupidity and intelligence. Me, for example, I am the most intelligent man on the road.

THE MOTHER: What do you mean?

THE BABY: Why?

THE SCHOLAR: Because I know how to read. And, to my knowledge, I am the only man who knows how to read.

THE MOTHER: What does that mean, read?

THE SCHOLAR: It means deciphering the signs that are written. The signs are in books. Look.

He shows his books.

THE MOTHER: What are these things? Where did you find them?

THE BABY: *(Sniffling the book.)* That doesn't smell good.

THE SCHOLAR: I find then in the 'shelters'. I search through the 'shelters' everywhere on my way, and sometimes, I find a book. So I take it and decipher it.

THE MOTHER: I don't understand.

THE SCHOLAR: The signs correspond to a sound. When you understand them, the book tells us a story, as if someone was talking to us from another world where we didn't exist yet. When I have read all the books, I will know the secret of the universe.

THE BABY: Do your books also talk about mammies?

THE SCHOLAR: They talk about everything.

THE MOTHER: Show us how your books talk.

THE SCHOLAR: With pleasure. Listen to what is written here. *(He takes a book, and reads out without expression.)* The earth was formless and empty. There was darkness on the surface of the abyss and the Spirit of God moved underneath the waters …

SCENE NINE

Enter a young girl who sits down and starts drawing something on the ground with her finger. THE SCHOLAR, MOTHER and BABY are still there. THE BABY starts to cry.

THE MOTHER: Why are you crying? What's with you?

THE BABY: I am afraid. *(He jumps around her neck.)* It scares me what he's reading.

THE MOTHER: Me too. *(She pulls the BABY closer towards her.)* Even when I don't understand any of it.

THE SCHOLAR: *(Continues to read.)* God says: Let there be light! And there was light. God saw the light was good; and God separated the light from darkness.

THE BABY slips out of the arms of THE MOTHER and goes towards the girl who's drawing, and who we will call 'THE PAINTER'.

THE BABY: What are you doing?

THE PAINTER: I'm drawing. Shush!

THE BABY: *(To THE MOTHER.)* She is drawing, what does that mean?

THE MOTHER: I don't know.

THE PAINTER: There you go, it's done. Come and look.

THE MOTHER: I don't see anything.

THE BABY: What is it?

THE PAINTER: A horse.

THE BABY: What is a horse?

THE PAINTER: I don't know. It's a shape born in my head. All the time, all sorts of shapes are born in my head, and I draw them, and it's beautiful.

THE BABY: Yes, it's beautiful.

THE MOTHER: But there is nothing at all. I'm meeting nothing but crazy people today, I'm going.

THE BABY: Can I come with you?

THE MOTHER: If you want. But I'm not carrying you. And stop sucking your thumb. *(While leaving, to THE BABY.)* Did you see something?

THE BABY: Yes, I saw a beautiful horse.

THE MOTHER: Liar!

THE MOTHER and THE BABY exit

THE PAINTER: Come and see, sir, how beautiful it is.

THE SCHOLAR: What is beautiful?

THE PAINTER: My drawing, the horse, here.

THE SCHOLAR: I don't see anything, as a result, it's not beautiful. On the other hand, this is beautiful. The eternal God made man out of the dust of the earth. He blew in his nostrils a breath of life and man became a living soul.

THE PAINTER: Look! There! What is he doing?

SCENE TEN

Someone arrives from the left side. That is to say, he's walking in the wrong direction. THE SCHOLAR and THE PAINTER look at him, stunned.

THE SCHOLAR: Halt! Halt! Stop!

THE GAINSAYER: Why?

THE PAINTER: You are not walking in the right direction.

THE GAINSAYER: Why? Is there a right and a wrong direction?

THE SCHOLAR: Yes, this road leads that way. And the other leads that way.

THE GAINSAYER: That doesn't mean anything. You walk, that's it.

THE PAINTER: If you want to walk in that direction, you have to take the other road.

THE GAINSAYER: Why?

THE PAINTER: Because.

THE SCHOLAR: You just have to cross the borderline and you're on your way.

THE GAINSAYER: Here as well, I am on my way. I am everywhere on my way.

THE PAINTER: You are walking backwards.

THE GAINSAYER: Not at all. I'm walking against the grain.

THE SCHOLAR: That's not done.

THE GAINSAYER: It is. Since I am doing it.

THE SCHOLAR: It's forbidden. Did nobody ever tell you that it is forbidden?

THE GAINSAYER: They did. They don't stop telling me.

THE PAINTER: Then why are you not changing lanes?

THE GAINSAYER: Why would I change? Because they tell me?

THE PAINTER: Yes, because they tell you.

THE GAINSAYER: I like walking the wrong way.

He wants to step forward, but THE PAINTER stops him.

THE PAINTER: Careful! You're stepping on my drawing.

THE SCHOLAR: You walk on the right side. It's the law.

THE GAINSAYER: I don't like the law.

THE SCHOLAR: That's anarchy!

THE PAINTER: *(To THE SCHOLAR.)* Come, we'll put him on the other lane.

THE PAINTER and THE SCHOLAR lift THE GAINSAYER and put him on the other lane.)

THE PAINTER: There you go. Now you can walk that way.

THE GAINSAYER: Having thought about it, I don't feel like it anymore.

He goes left again, in the wrong direction.

THE SCHOLAR: You are going in the wrong way.

THE GAINSAYER: I don't give a damnway!

THE PAINTER: What an idiot. I'm going to draw a bird.

She draws on the ground.

THE SCHOLAR: And I am going back to my reading.

He looks in his book. A disquieting sound makes itself heard.

THE SCHOLAR: ... 'but you shall not eat from the tree of knowledge of good and evil, for on the day you eat from it, you shall surely die.' *(Lifting his head.)* I am afraid!

SCENE ELEVEN

A wild gang of 5-6 characters move over the road. The word 'afraid' is picked up by the rest of the actors.

MURMURS AND SHOUTS: Afraid ... afraid ... Afraid ... The Wild Ones ... The Wild Ones attack ...

The walk of the actors becomes a run. 'THE WILD ONES' advance, banging blindly, left and right, with metal scrap snatched from cars and sign posts

THE WILD ONES: We are violence. Anger, fury, madness. We are the Wild Ones. Wild and beautiful, barbaric, cruel, ferocious, inhuman. We are the fear, the dread, the panic, the terror. We want to shatter, slash, ravage, destroy, slaughter, annihilate, crush, exterminate, massacre, kill.

THE WILD ONES arrive close to THE SCHOLAR and THE PAINTER.

THE PAINTER: Don't walk on my drawings! Don't walk on my drawings! Oh, horrible!

She flees.

THE SCHOLAR tries to gather his books, but THE WILD ONES surround him.

THE SCHOLAR: It is the apocalypse!

THE WILD ONES knock him down and drag him towards a sign that says: 'DEAD END.' The books stay there, scattered over the ground. Nothing is heard but the panting of those still running.

SCENE TWELVE

A YOUNG GIRL arrives from one side, a young man from the other /In the opposite direction, on the other lane). Still out of breath, they slow down, stop at the same time, look at each other. While looking at each other they 'fly' one towards the other, 'in slow motion'. A barrier separates them.

THE YOUNG MAN: What sparkles in your eyes?

THE GIRL: The same light as in yours. I don't know what it is.

THE YOUNG MAN: It hurts.

THE GIRL: Yes, and at the same time …

THE YOUNG MAN: It is wonderful.

THE GIRL: Yes.

They come one step closer, together. THE YOUNG MAN holds out his hand.

THE YOUNG MAN: Give me your hand.

THE GIRL places her hand in that of THE YOUNG MAN.

THE GIRL: Your hand burns my palm.

THE YOUNG MAN: My whole body embraces you.

THE GIRL: I am thirsty. I don't see anything else but your lips. Give me something to drink.

They slowly fold their arms, and bring their heads closer.

THE YOUNG MAN: What force pulls us?

THE GIRL: What miracle is happening to us?

They embrace for a long time. From off stage there's some ironic whistling.

THE YOUNG MAN: Nothing or nobody will pull me away from you.

THE GIRL: It will, sadly. The road. It takes you that way, and me this way.

THE YOUNG MAN: Cursed be the road that separates us.

THE GIRL: Mine will be drenched with tears.

THE YOUNG MAN: Mine dark and goalless.

THE GIRL: I will never forget you.

THE YOUNG MAN: I will only think of you.

OFF STAGE VOICE: And so on, and so on. The usual lover's vows.

THE GIRL: Maybe our roads will meet again.

THE YOUNG MAN: One day, who knows?

OFF STAGE VOICE: On the road everything is possible. But unlikely and never certain.

THE GIRL: We have to walk. Good bye… Good bye …

THE YOUNG MAN: Fare well, fare well …

Very slowly they let go, and walk looking back, up to the exit where they say together.

THE GIRL AND THE YOUNG MAN: Fare well … love …

SCENE THIRTEEN

THE SUIT still walks on alone, somewhere on the road.

THE SUIT: Getting lost on a highway! And that happens to me, to me! Engineer of bridges and roads. First price of the 'South-West competition.' On foot on a highway! Highways are not made for pedestrians. They are most certainly to be advised against for pedestrians. On foot, it's too long, too tiring. Try walking on a highway! It seems you are getting lost in infinity. It drives you mad. All that grey … all that concrete … Its crossings, its bends, its junctions, its interchanges, its forks, its exits that bring you to another road. It's a nightmare, it can't be anything but a nightmare … *(Pause.)* I'll never get off it. I'll never get away from it. I will die here, like a dog. There aren't even any dogs. I will die here like a poor … pedestrian.

What's that? *(He picks up a book.)* It's the Bible. I am going to pray. There's nothing left but to pray. *(He holds the Bible to his heart.)* My Lord! Help me! If you get me out of here, this spider's web, this concrete labyrinth, I promise to never construct even the smallest road. Not even a tiny little street. Nothing absolutely nothing. I won't even clear the snow in winter. I'll change profession. I'll recycle myself. I'll become … a monk or a gardener … Yes, a monk gardener. I will cultivate the earth. 'Let us cultivate our garden.' Who said that? Voltaire, maybe. He was right. The environmentalists are right. I detested them, I forgive them. They are a thousand times right. We must save nature. Man's natural environment. The trees, the forests, the lakes, the rivers, the valleys, the mountains and the marshes.

A bit of green, my Lord, do a miracle, a bit of green!

A sign lights up, shaped as an arrow: 'Miracle'.

SCENE FOURTEEN

The road is broken up. Pieces of cement lay around a spot of green with a tree in the middle. A man, standing next to the tree, talks to a few people. We will call the man, 'THE MAD MAN', because that is what he is to the others.

THE MAD MAN: The roots stayed alive under the concrete. The roots shattered the concrete. I was sitting there, next to the woman that I loved, and who had passed away. I wanted to die myself. I didn't feel like walking anymore. I saw a crack in the concrete, something white came from it. It was a root, I tasted it, it was good. So I broke the concrete with a piece of iron, and I found earth. I dug a hole, in there I put the woman I loved, I covered her with earth, and grass started to grow.

NO1: Why did you put that woman in the ground?

THE MAD MAN: So nobody would touch her.

NO2: That's not nice that. You should have left her for us, and found yourself another one, a living one.

THE MAD MAN: I loved her. I didn't want another.

NO3: It's not grey here. It's another colour.

THE MAD MAN: It's green. It's the colour of grass. And this is a tree.

NO4: What is that good for?

THE MAD MAN: It's nice to look at and it bears fruit.

He shows an apple.

NO1: What is that?

THE MAD MAN: It is good to eat.

NO2: That would surprise me.

THE MAD MAN: Who wants to try?

NO3: Nobody is crazy enough. Me, I'm off.

NO4: Me too.

THE MAD MAN: For years, people stopped, they looked, and then went on.

NO1: That's life. You have to walk.

NO2: It's stronger than us.

NO3: Have to look for the exit.

THE MAD MAN: It is here the exit. Stay here. Help me to break the concrete. If everyone puts himself too it, the road will disappear and the earth will be green again.

NO4: He is crazy!

ALL: Let's go.

They leave. THE MAD MAN starts to break the concrete again. A ray of sunlight lights up the top of the tree. Enter THE SAD WOMAN.)

THE SAD WOMAN: What is that? It's horrible! Oh, my eyes! I'm hurt!

THE MAD MAN: It's the sun. My tree has broken through the fog

THE SAD WOMAN: Help! Help! I'm going blind!

She runs off, covering her eyes.

SCENE FIFTEEN

THE SUIT arrives before the tree and THE MAD MAN.

THE SUIT: A Miracle! An oasis in the dessert. Or is it just an illusion?

THE MAD MAN places a sign on the border of the grass. 'IT IS FORBIDDEN TO WALK ON THE GRASS.'

THE SUIT: Forbidden? I would so love to … touch the grass, sit down on it… at the foot of the tree … You have apples! Apples! I am so thirsty … To eat an apple, it's … it's paradise!

THE MAD MAN: Yes. It's my own personal paradise. Each his own. This one is forbidden to you. Your own paradise is the road. Your road. Your project, Mr Dubéton.

THE SUIT: But my road, my project is not made for pedestrians. They are made for powerful cars, fast, driving at 160, 200 km an hour.

THE MAD MAN: In our world these things don't exist. You go about on your road without a car, on foot, till the end of time, for eternity.

THE SUIT: Amen, I mean … this is not paradise, this is hell.

THE MAD MAN: That depends on your point of view. It's your business. I don't know anything about that. Move on! Move on!

Total darkness. You can hear the voice of THE SUIT. 'I want to wake up, I want to wake up. I have to wake up!' When the light returns, THE SUIT sits in a car seat, eyes wide open, then his eyes close and his head falls on his chest. You can hear the taa-tuu, taa-tuu of an ambulance.

Post Scriptum:

Laureat of the South West Competition. Mr Edmund Dubéton, a very talented engineer, died in a traffic accident.

'To honour his memory, his genius project will be realised without any changes.' Declared the Mayor, emotionally.

THE EPIDEMIC

Characters

THE DOCTOR (A WOMAN)

THE SAVIOUR

THE SAVED GIRL

FIRE FIGHTER 1

FIRE FIGHTER 2

THE CONVINCER

MAN 1

MAN 2

MALABAR

DOCTOR, SAVIOUR, SAVED GIRL.

The set represents a doctor's office, rather neglected. The DOCTOR sits at her desk. It is a woman. She is in her fifties, aged rather badly ... A bottle of red wine stands before her.

THE DOCTOR: Clouds. Nothing but clouds. None of those rubbish sunsets, orange and all that. I hate the beautiful things of nature. What I like is shit weather. Rain, mist, wind, mud, shit, in other words.

She pours a drink. She drinks.

To my health. I hate health. Wine is very bad for your health and so is smoking.

She lights a cigarette.

It can be so long ... No patients. Nobody. No sick people. Only dead ones. What are they anyway, sick people? A damn nuisance. People need to be in good health, or they might as well croak. Take care of them? Heal them? What for? There's too many.

She drinks.

Medicine, don't make me laugh. It's just good to fix a sore throat. But a sore throat, that can heal by itself.

She drinks.

It's so quite. I wonder if it will snow ... I wonder why I wonder about that. That it snows or not ... Anyway, I wonder why I still wonder about anything anyway.

Someone knocks at the door.

THE DOCTOR: Get pampered somewhere else. I don't care. I don't care about your sore throat. That'll heal by itself.

Another knock, harder.

Take an aspirin. It's the absolute remedy. It's good for everything. If that doesn't work, nothing will.

Another knock, harder still.

Alright, alright. I can inject you with antibiotics. They're good as well, antibiotics. It destroys the microbes, the viruses, the germs, destroys everything. Can get it orally, a prick in the buttocks, intravenous …

The door bursts opens. The SAVIOUR enters, carrying in his arms a young girl that he delicately places on the doctor's bench. He wipes his forehead.

THE DOCTOR: What is that?

THE SAVIOUR: It's a girl, a beautiful young girl I found hanging in the forest.

THE DOCTOR: Is that all you found?

THE SAVIOUR: What do you mean, is that all? I wasn't looking for mushrooms.

THE DOCTOR: What were you looking for?

THE SAVIOUR: A tree, to urinate. That's what I was looking for.

THE DOCTOR: A tree, that's not very difficult to find, in a forest.

THE SAVIOUR: No, it's not very … But, by Jove! We are talking away while…

THE DOCTOR: By Jove! Did you say, by Jove?

THE SAVIOUR: Yes, but, what's wrong with you?

THE DOCTOR: I love, "by Jove". It's an expression I love. You don't hear it often enough, unfortunately. By Jove! Hi, hi.

THE SAVIOUR: Will you just do something for this young girl!

THE DOCTOR: There weren't any others?

THE SAVIOUR: Other what?

THE DOCTOR: People hanging, in the forest.

THE SAVIOUR: I don't know. It is the only one I saw, and that I … saved. Why? Should there be others?

THE DOCTOR: The forest is full of them, full of people hanging themselves. Obviously, people only see the young and beautiful ones. It's always the same ones they save. Never an old one, ugly, dribbling, never!

THE SAVIOUR: But she was the only one I saw. I would have saved anyone!

THE DOCTOR: That's stupid, that. You shouldn't save just anyone. Anyway, you don't have the right to save anyone anyway.

THE SAVIOUR: What do you mean by that? It's not a right, it's an obligation.

THE DOCTOR: Trala lala laa. So what?

THE SAVIOUR: You have to save her, absolutely, completely. Give her back to life, to the future!

THE DOCTOR: She's a stiff.

THE SAVIOUR: No, she's not. She's breathing. You are a doctor, aren't you?

THE DOCTOR: I was. I was. But I don't have any sick people left, only dead ones, and sore throats. It's because of this wet weather. Would you like a drink?

THE DOCTOR gets up and starts rinsing a glass.

THE SAVIOUR: No, no. Thank you. Just do something for this charming young person.

THE DOCTOR: Charming, charming… It is always the pretty women that…

THE SAVIOUR: Do you think that I saw she was pretty? She had her tongue hanging out. She was completely blue.

THE DOCTOR: That's disgusting. *(Looking at the saved girl.)* She isn't blue anymore, now.

THE SAVIOUR: Exactly. She is still alive. Her heart is beating.

THE DOCTOR: We can't rely on the beats of the heart.

THE SAVIOUR grabs the DOCTOR by her shirt.

THE SAVIOUR: If you don't do something immediately, I'll smash your dirty mouth!

THE DOCTOR: Calm down. Calm down.

THE SAVIOUR: Examine her, at least.

THE DOCTOR: If you insist.

THE DOCTOR examines the YOUNG GIRL.

THE DOCTOR: Regular breathing, heartbeats, all very reassuring ... Oh, very nice titties!

THE SAVIOUR: Hey? What are you doing?

THE DOCTOR: Examining her of course. You wanted me to examine her. Isn't youth beautiful!

The SAVIOUR pushes the DOCTOR away.

THE SAVIOUR: Don't touch her anymore! Is there a clinic around here?

THE DOCTOR: No clinic, no hospital. Just me around here. Look, she's opening her eyes!

The SAVIOUR approaches the SAVED GIRL.

THE SAVIOUR: Beautiful blue eyes. They are wonderful.

THE DOCTOR: Earlier, her whole body was blue. You didn't think that was wonderful, did you?

THE SAVIOUR: You witch. I'm taking her away immediately.

THE SAVED GIRL: I don't want to be taken away. I'm good here, lying down. I'm very good.

THE DOCTOR: You see?

THE SAVED GIRL: Where am I? Is this it, the other world?

THE DOCTOR giggles.

THE SAVIOUR: No, you're still on earth. You are alive. It's me who saved you.

THE SAVED GIRL: What an ass!

THE SAVIOUR: I'm sorry?

THE DOCTOR: Yes, you heard it right. She said: what an ass!

THE SAVED GIRL: Egoist, hypocrite, moron, introvert, foetus.

THE SAVIOUR: Me?

THE DOCTOR: You, to a T.

THE SAVIOUR: Why?

THE SAVED GIRL: Because!

THE DOCTOR: Because you got involved in something that didn't concern you.

THE SAVIOUR: Me? When? How?

THE SAVED GIRL: I want to sleep now.

THE SAVIOUR: She seems to be getting better.

THE DOCTOR: You see? She recovered by herself. As usual.

THE SAVIOUR: As usual? What do I do now?

THE DOCTOR: You have to let her sleep.

THE SAVIOUR: Yes, I'll wait.

THE SAVED GIRL: Don't bother. I can sleep very well alone.

THE DOCTOR: You could go and inform the authorities while you're waiting.

THE SAVIOUR: Is there a phone?

THE DOCTOR: The phone doesn't work.

THE SAVIOUR: Is there anything that works in this shithole?

THE DOCTOR: Nothing, nothing works.

THE SAVIOUR: But why, good God ...

THE DOCTOR: You could have said, "by Jove", instead of ...

THE SAVIOUR: What is going on here, really?

THE DOCTOR: Nothing special. Almost everyone is dead. All suicide.

THE SAVIOUR: Almost everyone? But ... why?

THE DOCTOR: Don't known. No reason. It's an epidemic.

THE SAVIOUR: An epidemic ... of suicides?

THE DOCTOR: Yes. Microbes, a suicide virus. Epidemic.

THE DOCTOR takes two glasses, offers one to the SAVIOUR.

THE DOCTOR: You don't want some?

THE SAVIOUR: What are you drinking?

THE DOCTOR: A rough red, local. I've got the cellar full. You want some? It's not very good.

THE SAVIOUR: You've got nothing else? A ... a strong drink?

THE DOCTOR: Hi, hi. There is nothing else. You drink that, or nothing.

THE SAVIOUR takes a glass and drinks, pulling a face.

THE SAVIOUR: So what authorities do we have to inform?

THE DOCTOR: The committee of suicides. It interests them each time one of them is saved.

THE SAVIOUR: And in the others they are not interested?

THE DOCTOR: They are. They examine them all, to see if they are really dead. But what interests them most are the saved ones.

THE SAVIOUR: Why?

THE DOCTOR: To ask them questions. They can't do that with the dead ones.

THE SAVIOUR: And where is that committee?

THE SAVIOUR: In the pub opposite. It's the firemen who take care of that.

THE SAVIOUR: The firemen?

THE DOCTOR: Yes, the firemen. They're very good. Stupid, but efficient. In the beginning, they send us psychiatrists, but they all killed themselves.

THE SAVIOUR: The psychiatrists?

THE DOCTOR: Yeah. Does that surprise you? There were eight. The firemen never kill themselves, and they're extremely well organised. By the way, how did you get into this shithole?

THE SAVIOUR: By car. I took a wrong turn at a junction. I don't even know where I am.

THE DOCTOR: Better for you. Our hole is in quarantine. Nobody gets in, nobody gets out. Traffic is diverted. You didn't see a roadblock?

THE SAVIOUR: No, nothing, why?

THE DOCTOR: Nobody can come in here, because of the epidemic.

THE SAVIOUR: And what do you do for food?

THE DOCTOR: It's the firemen who go find it right at the roadblock.

THE SAVIOUR: I'm telling you again, I didn't see a roadblock.

THE DOCTOR: Bizarre. Anyway, you'll see it on your way out, but then, you shouldn't even think of getting out

THE SAVIOUR: What? I can't leave from here? I have business to attend to, I have responsibilities.

THE DOCTOR: Yeah, yeah.

THE SAVIOUR: What? Yeah, yeah.

THE DOCTOR: Nothing. You are contaminated now by the suicide virus. If you would leave here, you'll contaminate the whole country. The world! Go and find the firemen.

THE SAVIOUR: And what are they going to do?

THE DOCTOR: Death certificate.

THE SAVIOUR: She isn't dead!

THE DOCTOR: An interrogation then.

THE SAVIOUR: The firemen?

THE DOCTOR: Yes, the firemen. Interrogation, psychoanalysis, even autopsies. They take themselves for our good God, these firemen.

THE SAVIOUR: They should still let me go.

THE DOCTOR: No way. But if it is true that there is no more roadblock...

THE SAVIOUR: Nothing.

THE DOCTOR: They must be all hanging in the forest ... or asphyxiated with the gas of their cars, or ... shot ...

THE SAVIOUR: Who are you talking about?

THE DOCTOR: The roadblock cops. The cops are as stupid as the firemen, but they are more sensitive.

THE SAVIOUR: You must be confused, sensitive, cops?

THE DOCTOR: And how! They are visionaries, martyrs, frustrated, guilt ridden. They terribly lack affection.

THE SAVIOUR: That is very touching. No more roadblock then! And the only ones left are the firemen. I'll go and get them. Where can I find them at this hour?

THE DOCTOR: In the pub opposite. I already told you.

THE SAVIOUR: Is it still open?

THE DOCTOR: It's always open.

THE SAVIOUR bends over the SAVED GIRL, looks at her lovingly.

THE SAVIOUR: She sleeps like an angel. In two minutes I'll be back, and I'll leave with her, far from here.

THE DOCTOR: With her? That would surprise me.

THE SAVIOUR: I love her.

THE DOCTOR: Ah!

THE SAVIOUR: Yes. Nothing will stop me.

THE DOCTOR: Oh love! I was young and beautiful too.

THE SAVIOUR: Impossible!

THE DOCTOR: Like everyone else. And she as well, one day, she will …

THE SAVIOUR: Not in a long time.

THE DOCTOR: If you knew how fast time goes by!

THE SAVIOUR: I'll better go and look for the firemen.

THE DOCTOR: Yes, you do that. You do that.

THE SAVIOUR exits.

SCENE TWO

THE DOCTOR, THE SAVED GIRL.

THE SAVED GIRL: Is he gone, that ass?

THE DOCTOR: Finally, yes.

THE SAVED GIRL gets up.

THE SAVED GIRL: Do you have a drink for me?

THE DOCTOR: Of course.

THE DOCTOR fills the glass the SAVIOUR was drinking from. She passes it on to THE SAVED GIRL. The two women drink.

THE SAVED GIRL: At the end I thought you were going to cry over your youth.

Long silence. THE SAVED GIRL strolls around with her glass.

THE SAVED GIRL: You like that?

THE DOCTOR: I don't ask myself questions. I drink what there is.

THE SAVED GIRL: I'm not talking about the wine. It's undrinkable. I am talking about the silence.

THE DOCTOR: About silence in general?

THE SAVED GIRL: No, our silence in particular.

THE DOCTOR: Yeah, I like it. It has a quality… a silent quality in particular.

THE SAVED GIRL: Not anymore now. Stop rambling!

THE DOCTOR: Because I ramble?

THE SAVED GIRL: And because you forget to pour.

THE SAVED GIRL pours the wine. Silence.

THE SAVED GIRL: So, it's happening?

THE DOCTOR: What?

THE SAVED GIRL: We can't stay here, forever, together.

THE DOCTOR: Yes, I'm leaving.

THE DOCTORS opens the window.

THE SAVED GIRL: Is there something that interests you outside?

THE DOCTOR: No, nothing. What could interest me outside?

THE SAVED GIRL: Then close the window. It's cold.

THE DOCTOR: It's cold? When? Here? Outside?

THE SAVED GIRL: Your act is becoming monotonous. It is always the same.

THE DOCTOR: So is yours. I'm giving you my calendar. Here!

THE SAVED GIRL: For what? To know what day it is?

THE DOCTOR: It's Tuesday.

THE SAVED GIRL: What's the point?

THE DOCTOR: No point, exactly. Could still come in handy. Feel free to smoke, while you're waiting.

THE DOCTOR climbs into the window.

THE SAVED GIRL: You risk breaking something if you jump.

THE DOCTOR: It's that what bothers me. We're not high enough. But what if I dive?

THE SAVED GIRL: You can always try.

THE DOCTOR dives from the window. Sound of a crash, silence. THE SAVED GIRL pours herself a drink, sits in THE DOCTOR's chair.

THE SAVED GIRL: She dived. And it's Tuesday. As usual.

THE SAVED GIRL drinks, she lights a cigarette.

THE SAVED GIRL: She really dived. She's outside, outside of it all. Life always ends in the same way.

The sirens of the firemen. THE SAVED GIRL quickly puts on a white blouse.

SCENE THREE

THE SAVED GIRL, FIRE FIGHTER 1, FIRE FIGHTER 2, THE SAVIOUR.

FIREMEN 1 and 2, enter.

FIRE FIGHTER 1: Hello, Doctor.

FIRE FIGHTER 2: The suicide? Where is she?

THE SAVED GIRL: She just jumped out of the window.

FIRE FIGHTER 1: Ah well, she wasn't saved then?

FIRE FIGHTER 2: I'll go and see if she's really dead.

FIRE FIGHTER 2 exits. THE SAVIOUR enters.

THE SAVIOUR: Where is that fire fighter running to? Where's the doctor?

FIRE FIGHTER 1: Is that not her, the doctor?

THE SAVIOUR: No, that's who I saved.

FIRE FIGHTER 1: Really! So, you're the Doctor?

THE SAVIOUR: No, I'm not. Where is she?

FIRE FIGHTER 1: Then who jumped out of the window?

THE SAVIOUR: Someone jumped out of the window? But that's dangerous! We're on the second floor!

THE SAVED GIRL: She didn't jump. She dived.

FIRE FIGHTER 1: Dived, who?

THE SAVIOUR: Dived? But then! …

THE SAVED GIRL: Oh yes! Anyway, I'm off. I'm going home.

FIRE MAN 1: There is no more 'home'.

THE SAVIOUR: One moment, one moment. I'm responsible for you. I saved your life.

FIRE FIGHTER 1: Was she ill?

THE SAVED GIRL: Me, ill?

THE SAVIOUR: No, I took her down. I still have her rope in my pocket.

THE SAVED GIRL: That'll bring you luck.

FIRE FIGHTER 1: That's not your job. We take people down.

THE SAVIOUR: Oh really! By drinking in the pub? You take a few down, do you?

FIRE FIGHTER 1: That's down to the weather. What the weather is like.

THE SAVIOUR: But where is the doctor gone?

THE SAVED GIRL: Through the window.

THE SAVIOUR: The doctor jumped out of the window? Why?

THE SAVED GIRL: To kill herself of course.

FIRE FIGHTER 1: So, it's him … it's her, it's the doctor who jumped out of the window? And you, you've been saved, then.

THE SAVED GIRL: That's right.

FIRE FIGHTER 1: Ah, good. So, now, we've got to get the Convincer.

THE SAVIOUR: Who?

FIRE FIGHTER 1: The Convincer, who convinces.

THE SAVIOUR: Who convinces who?

FIRE FIGHTER 1: Her, he will convince her!

THE SAVED GIRL: Of what?

FIRE FIGHTER 1: Of the uselessness of things. Sorry. Of suicide. Of non suicide. Yes, that's it. To stop hanging yourself.

THE SAVIOUR: Where is he, this man?

FIRE FIGHTER 1: It is not a man. It's a Convincer. He used to be a psychiatrist.

THE SAVIOUR: I thought you didn't have any left.

FIRE FIGHTER: He was the last one. We've appointed him Convincer.

SCENE FOUR

THE SAVIOUR, THE SAVED GIRL, FIRE FIGHTER 1, FIRE FIGHTER 2. MAN 1, MAN 2, THE DOCTOR (as a corpse).

FIRE FIGHTER 2 enters, followed by MAN 1 and 2, carrying the DOCTOR on a stretcher.

FIRE FIGHTER 2: Put the stretcher there, in the corner.

THE SAVIOUR: I hope it's not serious, that we can save her.

THE SAVED GIRL: There's nothing left to save. She dived.

MAN 1: She landed on her head.

The two men put the stretcher down without much care.

THE SAVIOUR: Even then … she isn't dead, is she?

MAN 2: Proper dead.

THE SAVIOUR: Maybe her heart still beats. If the heart's fine, all is good.

THE SAVIOUR bends over the corpse and lifts the cloth that covers it.

THE SAVIOUR: But … there's almost nothing left of her head.

FIRE FIGHTER 1: So, it's the doctor who is the suicide, is that it?

FIRE FIGHTER 1 installs himself at the desk with some sheets of paper he pulled from his case.

FIRE FIGHTER 2: *(To the two men.)* You can leave now, thank you.

MAN 1: Thank you? Just like that? As simple as that?

MAN 2: Carrying a dead person up to the second floor! And "you can leave now, thank you".

MAN 1: On top of that, she was proper heavy.

THE SAVIOUR: What do they want?

THE SAVED GIRL: Cash, of course.

THE SAVIOUR: They want money?

THE SAVED GIRL: What else would they want? They did their job, no?

THE SAVIOUR gives the two men a note.

MAN 1: Thank you, sir. You are a kind man.

MAN 2: Thank you, sir. You are one of a kind.

FIRE FIGHTER 2: And send me the Convincer, straight away! He must be in the pub.

MAN 1: We'll tell him.

MAN 2: Sure to send him.

MAN 1 and 2 exit.

SCENE FIVE

FIREMEN 1, FIRE FIGHTER 2, THE SAVIOUR, THE SAVED GIRL, THE DOCTOR (Corpse).

FIRE FIGHTER 1: Shall we cut her up here?

FIRE FIGHTER 2: What for? She's enough of a mess as it is.

FIRE FIGHTER 1: What shall we do with her?

FIRE FIGHTER 2: We'll leave her where she is. We're not in a hurry.

FIRE FIGHTER 1: By the way, why did the doctor jump?

THE SAVED GIRL: Oh, she does that every time she sees me. Well, I'm off.

THE SAVIOUR: No, no! I'm responsible for you.

FIRE FIGHTER 2: You have to wait for the Convincer.

THE SAVED GIRL: Is that mandatory?

FIRE FIGHTER 2: You could say that. Anyway, we've got nothing else to do tonight.

FIRE FIGHTER 1: While we're waiting, we could do our report.

FIRE FIGHTER 2: What report?

FIRE FIGHTER 1: On her. The one who's not dead.

FIRE FIGHTER 2: You're obsessed with reports. She hung
    herself and someone took her down.

THE SAVIOUR: It was me who …

FIRE FIGHTER 1: Shut up. Question number 1: Cause?

THE SAVED GIRL: What do you mean, cause?

FIRE FIGHTER 1: I don't know. That's what it says here: cause.
    So, the cause.

THE SAVED GIRL: The cause of what? Of the rescue?

FIRE FIGHTER 1: No, of the hanging. The why of the hanging.

THE SAVED GIRL: To die.

FIRE FIGHTER 1: Why die?

THE SAVED GIRL: I had enough.

FIRE FIGHTER 1: Of what?

THE SAVED GIRL: Of firemen.

*The SAVED GIRL pours herself a drink and sits down, comfortably
on the couch.*

FIRE FIGHTER 1: Is she trying to upset us?

FIRE FIGHTER 2: It doesn't matter.

FIRE FIGHTER 1: That's true. So, basically, I can just put
    anything in my report.

THE SAVED GIRL: Who's the report for?

FIRE FIGHTER 1: For the questionnaire. Do I fill it in on my own?

FIRE FIGHTER 2: As usual.

FIRE FIGHTER 1: Then, as usual, it will be boring.

FIRE FIGHTER 2: Boring. Boring. You don't have to.

FIRE FIGHTER 1: I don't have to. That's easy to say.

*FIRE FIGHTER 1 writes. FIRE FIGHTER 2 shrugs his shoulders, then
to the SAVIOUR.*

FIRE FIGHTER 2: Where did you drop out from?

THE SAVIOUR: I didn't drop.

FIRE FIGHTER 2: That won't be long. Where did you leave from?

THE SAVIOUR: Exactly, I want to leave from this shit hole.

FIRE FIGHTER 2: That's not possible.

THE SAVIOUR: And Why?

FIRE FIGHTER 2: Because it's impossible.

THE SAVIOUR: I see.

FIRE FIGHTER 2: You don't see anything at all.

THE SAVIOUR: I do. Her. Maybe I am not seeing anything else, but I see her.

FIRE FIGHTER 2: It doesn't matter. She's just an illusion, completely illusive.

THE SAVIOUR: She doesn't look it.

FIRE FIGHTER 2: Ha, the look, that has nothing to do with these circumstances here.

THE SAVIOUR: What circumstances?

FIRE FIGHTER 2: Very particular circumstances.

SCENE SIX

THE PRECEDING and THE CONVINCER.

THE CONVINCER enters.

THE CONVINCER: Hello, it's me. Did you call for me?

FIRE FIGHTER 2: You took a long time to come. Were you away?

CONVINCER: I wasn't away. I was somewhere else.

FIRE FIGHTER 2: Why were you somewhere else?

THE SAVED GIRL: Because it's Tuesday.

CONVINCER: I didn't notice anything. So that's what it was? Thank you.

THE SAVIOUR: I don't get any of this. What does that do, a Tuesday?

THE SAVED GIRL: It's the last day before Wednesday. Get it?

CONVINCER: On top of that, I'm unwell.

FIRE FIGHTER 1: He is always unwell. Especially here, hey? The head.

CONVINCER: You cannot always be not unwell, morel.

FIRE FIGHTER 1: Morel, you talking to me or what?

CONVINCER: No, that was a rhyme.

FIRE FIGHTER 1: To get on my nerves, hey? That rhymes with nothing your mushroom.

FIRE FIGHTER 2: Alright. Alright. Here's someone who was saved, for you.

CONVINCER: Sex?

FIRE FIGHTER 1: Always sex. There's nothing else that interests them.

CONVINCER: The sex of the person who was saved?

FIRE FIGHTER 2: You don't see it?

CONVINCER: No. Luckily.

FIRE FIGHTER 2: Female.

CONVINCER: Single?

FIRE FIGHTER 2: I think so.

CONVINCER: You have to be certain. I take my profession seriously! I am aware of my responsibilities. You have appointed me Convincer, you will bear the consequences and the consequences will be serious, firemen, sirs, very serious, I mean to say with that, that …

FIRE FIGHTER 2: That's enough!

FIRE FIGHTER 1: What was he saying?

FIRE FIGHTER 2: Your marital status, miss?

THE SAVED GIRL: I'm single.

CONVINCER: Are you sure of that?

THE SAVED GIRL: Very much so.

THE SAVIOUR: That's good. Me too, I'm single.

CONVINCER: We're not talking about you. Not yet. Parents?

THE SAVED GIRL: Like everyone.

CONVINCER: What kind of parents?

THE SAVED GIRL: Father and mother.

CONVINCER: And the Holy Spirit? No, that's something else. The cause of suicide?

THE SAVED GIRL: Don't know.

THE SAVIOUR: It's ... maybe ... the epidemic.

CONVINCER: You again! We can't pin everything on the epidemic. On the other hand, why is there an epidemic? These are questions that lead very far. And because nobody can answer these questions, we simplify. "Cause unknown", that exists. Here, in the book.

THE CONVINCER takes a book from his pocket. He looks for a page. He reads aloud without conviction.

CONVINCER: Do not despair. Life is a source of happiness. Happiness is within reach of everyone. You have to enjoy life. You are young, the future is yours. Time will heal all wounds. Every winter is followed by a spring. Each illness has its ailment. You can still be a happy man, a happy woman. You ... find again ... place ... society ... fulfil ... duty. Engage yourself, have a goal ... fight ... result ... confidence in yourself ... optimistic ... success. Page eighty-four. Appendixes.

THE CONVINCER looks through his book.

CONVINCER: Here we are: Think of your parents. Do not cause them any serious grief.

FIRE FIGHTER 2: That's all?

CONVINCER: That's already not bad.

FIRE FIGHTER 2: Did you hear that?

THE SAVED GIRL: Oh! That! Yes! Quite a few times, already.

CONVINCER: There you go! Are you convinced?

THE SAVED GIRL: How could one not be?

FIRE FIGHTER 1: The report asks for a straight answer.

THE SAVED GIRL: I am absolutely convinced.

FIRE FIGHTER 1: Of what?

THE SAVED GIRL: Of anything you want.

FIRE FIGHTER 1: Well, that's alright then.

FIRE FIGHTER 2: You can go now.

THE SAVED GIRL: Where?

FIRE FIGHTER 2: Wherever you like.

THE SAVED GIRL: I can go back to the forest?

THE SAVIOUR: Hey, but, that's not right. I'll keep an eye on you now.

THE SAVED GIRL: Give me my rope back!

THE SAVIOUR: She's mad!

THE SAVED GIRL: It's my rope, isn't it?

CONVINCER: It's true, it's her rope!

THE SAVIOUR: I am responsible for you.

THE SAVED GIRL: But who does this guy think he is?

THE SAVIOUR: Come, we're going for a walk.

THE SAVED GIRL: Where?

THE SAVIOUR: Somewhere else. Far from here.

THE SAVED GIRL: To do what?

THE SAVIOUR: To do a whole lot of interesting things. Kissing you, for example.

THE SAVED GIRL: We haven't been introduced yet.

THE SAVIOUR: I love you.

THE SAVED GIRL: Just like that, all of a sudden, love at first sight, is it?

THE SAVIOUR: Yes. And for ever.

THE SAVED GIRL: *(If possible in a singing voice.)*
    And eternal love will take flight
    In a few days, in a few months
    In a few years and there will come another
    From somewhere, from nowhere and somewhere else
    And the wind sings about life and sings about love

And time haunts the anguish of death
And eternity passes by and passes by love
And passes by time and passes by life

Time plays with eternity
The clouds play with the sun
The lovers play with their hearts
Life plays with their love
And the wind sings about life and sing about love
And time haunts the anguish of death
And eternity passes by and passes by love
And passes by time and passes by life

THE SAVIOUR: Come darling.

THE SAVIOUR and the SAVED GIRL leave.

SCENE SEVEN

FIRE FIGHTER 1 and 2, CONVINCER, DOCTOR (Corpse).

FIRE FIGHTER 1, sobbing, tries to sing.

FIRE FIGHTER 1: And sing about life … about love … eternity … flies off … the anguish … death … it's beautiful, it's sad, it's wonderful.

FIRE FIGHTER 2: Are you mad or what?

CONVINCER: He's contaminated, that's all.

FIRE FIGHTER 1: Contaminated? Me? Say so, Convincer!

CONVINCER: So.

FIRE FIGHTER 1: What?

CONVINCER: You told me to say so, so I say so.

FIRE FIGHTER 1: He drives me mad.

CONVINCER: That would be redundant.

FIRE FIGHTER 2: Convincer! You haven't said much to that young girl.

CONVINCER: That was all there was on an unknown cause, here in the book. And now, I must retire from here, to somewhere else as quickly as possible.

FIRE FIGHTER 1: That's enough, understood? I'm fed up with your retirements, your somewhere elses and your Tuesdays, understood?

CONVINCER: There are also Thursdays. But less so.

FIRE FIGHTER 1: Less so? Thursdays?

FIRE FIGHTER 2: Leave it. You always fall for everything.

CONVINCER: He doesn't always fall. Sometimes he sits down, or sits up straight or lays down and …

THE CONVINCER notices the corpse.

CONVINCER: Oh well, did she jump again?

FIRE FIGHTER 1: Is that your business?

CONVINCER: When something is my business, I'll write you a letter. Goodbye! I need to get hold of that character, that Saviour.

THE CONVINCER wants to leave, but THE SAVIOUR enters with THE SAVED GIRL.

SCENE EIGHT

FIRE FIGHTER 1, FIRE FIGHTER 2, THE CONVINCER, THE DOCTOR (Corpse), THE SAVIOUR and THE SAVED GIRL.

THE SAVED GIRL: Let me go! Leave me alone.

THE SAVIOUR: Oh no, I won't leave you alone. She doesn't want me to stay with her.

CONVINCER: Then don't stay with her.

THE SAVIOUR: I am responsible for this young girl. I saved her life.

CONVINCER: So? You're not the only one.

THE SAVIOUR: I don't want her to attempt suicide a second time.

FIRE FIGHTER 2: She won't kill herself again. The Convincer has convinced her.

THE SAVIOUR: She wants to hang herself again. She told me.

THE SAVED GIRL: That was just to annoy you.

FIRE FIGHTER 1: Convincer, this is your fault. You didn't convince her very well.

CONVINCER: Listen, my little child. You are suffering from an Oedipus complex. You liken me to your father, who you always hated, like everyone does, and you are transferring your complex on to me, because to you, I appear to be a superior force.

FIRE FIGHTER 1: What did he say?

FIRE FIGHTER 2: It's the psychiatrist emerging. We did suppress it properly though.

FIRE FIGHTER 1: Enough. What do we do about it?

CONVINCER: I can read out once more, what I read out before.

THE CONVINCER looks through his book. Behind him the two Firemen are conspiring. FIRE FIGHTER 1 shows his gun. FIRE FIGHTER 2 gestures no. FIRE FIGHTER 1 shows a baton. FIRE FIGHTER 2 gestures yes.

FIRE FIGHTER 2: But properly, huh?

CONVINCER: Do not despair. Life is the source of happiness. Time will heal all wounds. All winters are followed by a spri …

FIRE FIGHTER 1 lifts his baton.

FIRE FIGHTER 1: Shall I?

FIRE FIGHTER 2: It looks necessary to me. I'd even say inevitable.

FIRE FIGHTER 1: What does that mean?

THE SAVIOUR: What are you going to do?

FIRE FIGHTER 2: Go!

CONVINCER: … Each pain has its remedy. You can still …

FIRE FIGHTER 1 hits. THE CONVINCER collapses.

FIRE FIGHTER 2: Is he stiff?

FIRE FIGHTER 1: Trust me.

THE SAVIOUR: You are … murderers.

THE SAVED GIRL: No, they're firemen.

FIRE FIGHTER 1: Do we cut him up?

FIRE FIGHTER 2: Tomorrow. Put him next to the other one.

FIRE FIGHTER 1: Put him. Put him … It's not a bundle of straw.

FIRE FIGHTER 2: I never said it was. Drag him in the corner then.

FIRE FIGHTER 1 drags the CONVINCER next to the DOCTOR.

THE SAVIOUR: I can't believe my eyes! Come, let's take my car and get out of here.

THE SAVED GIRL: Is that an obsession of yours or something?

THE SAVIOUR and THE SAVED GIRL leave.

SCENE NINE

FIRE FIGHTER 1, FIRE FIGHTER 2, MALABAR, MAN 1, MAN 2 and the corpses.

Enter MALABAR holding MAN 1 and 2 by the shoulder.

MALABAR: These two …

MAN 1 AND 2: Hello, everyone.

MALABAR: Are these your men?

FIRE FIGHTER 1: If you like …

FIRE FIGHTER 2: That's one way of putting it.

MALABAR: There's a little affair to sort out.

FIRE FIGHTER 2: What have you done now?

MALABAR: They ransacked my pub.

FIRE FIGHTER 1: I'm going to make a report.

FIRE FIGHTER 2: You'll be compensated. We'll take care of that.

MALABAR: I do hope so. If not, I close. No more pub, no more general headquarters, understood?

FIRE FIGHTER 2: Understood.

MALABAR: I trust you. You have always been good clients, you, firemen. So, I trust you. But be quick about it, huh. I give you my bills, and no quibbling, understood?

FIRE FIGHTER 2: Understood, all understood. Rest assured, we'll sort it here and now.

FIRE FIGHTER 1: Shall I make a report?

FIRE FIGHTER 2: If you feel like it …

FIRE FIGHTER 1: I feel like it.

MALABAR: Your report … what I do with that… I'll be right back for my money.

FIRE FIGHTER 2: Right, right.

Exit MALABAR.

SCENE TEN

FIRE FIGHTER 1, FIRE FIGHTER 2, MAN 1, MAN 2 and the CORPSES.

FIRE FIGHTER 2: What happened in the pub?

MAN 1: Well eh, we had a drink.

FIRE FIGHTER 2: One?

MAN 1: Well eh, let's say, two or three.

FIRE FIGHTER 2: Who bought them for you?

MAN 1: Ourselves. We had twenty quid.

FIRE FIGHTER 2: Who gave you the money?

MAN 1: You know alright. That man walking around with the bird.

FIRE FIGHTER 2: The Saviour of Souls? Oh well, he shouldn't have. Twenty quid, that's a lot. That's too much for you two.

MAN 2: For all that time we've been lugging corpses … And they never gave us anything!

FIRE FIGHTER 2: Let's move on, let's move on. So, you had three drinks. And after the third drink, what happened?

MAN 1: We still had a tenner left.

MAN 2: We wanted to split it up. He had to get change. We ordered another drink.

MAN 1: Then a second, because the first one tasted corked. We couldn't leave with that bad taste in the mouth. The second didn't taste corked. So we ordered a third one …

Pause.

FIRE FIGHTER 1: Go on!

MAN 1: We couldn't go on, we had no money left.

FIRE FIGHTER 2: What did you do then?

MAN 2: He, he threw a glass full in my face. Here.

MAN 1: So he, he took a chair and broke it on my head. I've got a bump, here.

MAN 2: Then, we threw and broke a whole load of things!

MAN 1: Yes! It was a terrible fight.

FIRE FIGHTER 1: Against who?

MAN 1: What do you mean, against who?

FIRE FIGHTER 1: Was there someone else in the pub?

MAN 1: I don't think so. Not that I remember. Except for the governor. He let us get on with it.

SCENE ELEVEN

THE PRECEDING, plus THE SAVIOUR and THE SAVED GIRL.

THE SAVIOUR enters with THE SAVED GIRL.

THE SAVED GIRL: What a bore that guy. He wants me to tell him my life story.

THE SAVIOUR: She's adorable. And the weather is changing. The sky is clear, there's an enormous moon. It's waning.

THE SAVED GIRL: It can wane or wax all it wants.

THE SAVED GIRL pours a drink and drinks.

THE SAVIOUR: You drink too much. It's not good for your health. And that wine is really bad, on top.

MAN 1: There's no such thing as a really bad wine.

THE SAVED GIRL: Why do you care? Take your car and shove off.

THE SAVED GIRL passes two glasses of wine to the two men.

THE SAVIOUR: Ah yes! My car! I can't find my car.

FIRE FIGHTER 1: What car?

THE SAVIOUR: My car. I parked it just in front of the house when I arrived. It's not there anymore.

FIRE FIGHTER 2: That's none of our business.

THE SAVIOUR: I have to find it.

FIRE FIGHTER 2: Nobody's stopping you.

THE SAVIOUR: You don't want to help me find it?

FIRE FIGHTER 2: We don't deal with cars. We have other stuff to do.

FIRE FIGHTER 1: We're dealing with the epidemic.

FIRE FIGHTER 2: It's a personal affair between you and your car. Us firemen, have nothing to do with that.

FIRE FIGHTER 1: I can make up a report if you like.

FIRE FIGHTER 2: Yes, make two or three! His car! Is this guy mad?

THE SAVIOUR: Well, I'm going to have another look. Are you coming with me, Miss?

THE SAVED GIRL: I walked enough for today.

THE SAVIOUR: I'll come back. Wait here for me.

THE SAVED GIRL: Of course. I'll wait for you. Biting my nails.

THE SAVIOUR goes off.

SCENE TWELVE

THE PRECEDING, without THE SAVIOUR.

FIRE FIGHTER 2: *(To the two men.)* So, to fix the damage you caused ...

MAN 1: What do we have to do?

MAN 2: At your service, sir.

FIRE FIGHTER 2: You go back to the pub, you have a strong coffee and you take this.

FIRE FIGHTER 2 holds out a gun towards the two men.

MAN 1: That, to pay with?

MAN 2: Why not? A piece like that, that's worth at least 200 quid.

FIRE FIGHTER 2: No. You take it to shoot.

MAN 1: At what? We already destroyed everything.

FIRE FIGHTER 2: Not at what. At who.

MAN 2: There's nobody left.

FIRE FIGHTER 2: There's the governor, no?

MAN 2: He's not such a bad fellow.

FIRE FIGHTER 2: So, then you pay for the damage. The bottles, the glasses, the chairs, the mirrors …

MAN 1: We don't have any money.

FIRE FIGHTER 2: That's why I am giving you the gun.

Again THE FIRE FIGHTER holds the gun out towards them, but the two men step back.

MAN 1: We don't know how to use it.

FIRE FIGHTER 1 takes the gun.

FIRE FIGHTER 1: It's not difficult. You pull here. *(A shot goes off.)* Sorry, did I wake someone up?

THE CONVINCER sits up.

CONVINCER: Yes, me. Do you have a cigarette?

FIRE FIGHTER 1 gives him a cigarette and gives him a light.

FIRE FIGHTER 1: That's what happens if you don't cut them up.

FIRE FIGHTER 2: That's what happens if you don't hit them properly. Right, you two. You are going to pay your debt with this gun, but first, do a round in the village to see if nothing moves.

CONVINCER: Believe you me, nothing's moving.

SCENE THIRTEEN

Preceding plus THE SAVIOUR.

THE SAVIOUR enters. He is beside himself.

THE SAVIOUR: It looks … It looks like … There's no more village … There are no more houses … There's no one … Nowhere.

THE SAVED GIRL: Did you find your car?

THE SAVIOUR: My car? No I didn't find it. I didn't find anything. There's nothing else but this house.

FIRE FIGHTER 2: And the pub?

THE SAVIOUR: Yes, the pub is there. But aside from that, nothing, nothing. Nothing!

THE SAVED GIRL: It looks like he's losing it.

THE SAVIOUR: Yes, I've gone mad. After seeing this vast plain, raked, without houses, without trees, without hills!

CONVINCER: Calm yourself. Haven't you ever seen an industrial zone?

THE SAVIOUR: Are you all crazy, or what? Madmen, assassins, killers!

FIRE FIGHTER 2: Easy, easy, be quiet! So, you two. You take care of the pub and do a round to see if there is anyone else.

MAN 1: And if there is someone else. What do we do?

FIRE FIGHTER 1: You pull here.

FIRE FIGHTER 2: Don't touch it! You'll wake the other one.

THE DOCTOR gets up.

DOCTOR: I'm so bashed up. My head hurts. Is there any red left?

THE DOCTOR finds the bottle, she drinks.

FIRE FIGHTER 2: You see?

FIRE FIGHTER 1: I didn't shoot though.

FIRE FIGHTER 2: Same difference.

FIRE FIGHTER 1: Because we didn't cut her up, her as well.

FIRE FIGHTER 2: Right, men, take the gun and do what I told you.

FIRE FIGHTER 2 forces MAN 1 to take the gun.

MAN 1: I don't really like it. It's not very funny.

MAN 2: Carrying corpses, alright, but making them …

CONVINCER: You're not going to play all delicate now, are you? Move, out!

THE CONVINCER pushes the two men towards the exit. They exit.

SCENE FOURTEEN

Preceding without the two men.

CONVINCER: *(To FIRE FIGHTER 1.)* You!

FIRE FIGHTER 1: Me!

CONVINCER: Take this small bomb. You will throw it in the pub. Those two characters need to be inside. And the governor, understood?

FIRE FIGHTER 1: At your service!

FIRE FIGHTER 1 exits with the bomb.

FIRE FIGHTER 2: And me, what do I do?

CONVINCER: I don't think we have anymore need for you. Thank you.

THE CONVINCER kills the fire fighter with one gunshot.

DOCTOR: Do we cut him up here?

All laugh madly, except THE SAVIOUR.

THE SAVIOUR: This isn't happening!

THE SAVED GIRL: Of course it isn't. And the other Fire fighter?

CONVINCER: He has to go off with his bomb.

THE SAVED GIRL: So, we're done.

THE SAVED GIRL disappears, CONVINCER installs himself comfortably.

CONVINCER: We just have to wait for the helicopter.

THE SAVIOUR: We can leave?

CONVINCER: Of course. What did you think?

THE SAVIOUR: With … all that has happened … I don't know anymore … it looks like a nightmare.

DOCTOR: It is one. It is one.

THE SAVIOUR: It looks like a nightmare, if it wasn't for … her. But … where is she? Is she gone?

CONVINCER: Who are you talking about, my poor boy?

THE SAVIOUR: That young girl … I saved … who was there …

DOCTOR: Ha ha! Hi hi! He means me.

THE SAVIOUR: No, not you! The young girl!

CONVINCER: He must have been seeing things.

THE SAVIOUR: It wasn't a hallucination. I touched her hair …
her blue eyes, I can still see them …

DOCTOR: Like mine?

THE SAVIOUR: No! *(Pause.)* Yes, a bit like yours. But where is she?

DOCTOR: Here. Aren't they beautiful, my blue eyes?

THE SAVIOUR: No, they are not beautiful!

DOCTOR: They're the same ones though. The eyes, it's all
that's left. The hair has gone grey, the face wrinkled, the
figure, let's not talk about that.

CONVINCER: Will that do, as explanation?

THE SAVIOUR: No, it won't do. Where is she?

DOCTOR: I'm here. There was no one else.

THE SAVIOUR: I'm going to look for her. I'll find her. I'll leave
with her. I'll leave this world of crazy people.

CONVINCER: That's exactly what we are going to do. You just
have to take the helicopter with us.

THE SAVIOUR: Not without her.

CONVINCER: But she is there. She has aged a bit, that's all.

DOCTOR: We're not going far. Just to the next village.

THE SAVIOUR: To do what?

CONVINCER: To spread the epidemic. You will be the first in
line.

THE SAVIOUR: What line?

THE DOCTOR: Of suicides. Come on. Don't you understand
anything then?

THE SAVIOUR: No. Nothing.

CONVINCER: We go from one village to another with a
contaminated person like you. He passes the virus to
everyone else, and when there is no one left, we level the
village. It's simple.

THE SAVIOUR: But … to what purpose?

CONVINCER: We have to make space. For factories, highways, sites of all sorts.

DOCTOR: The helicopter will be here in a moment or two.

CONVINCER: I am sorry, darling, there are only two seats in the helicopter.

DOCTOR: What do you mean?

CONVINCER: You're too much. You're redundant. We don't need you anymore. Thank you for your cooperation.

THE CONVINCER guns the DOCTOR down.

SCENE FIFTEEN

CONVINCER, THE SAVIOUR, MAN 1, MAN 2, THE SAVED GIRL.

MAN 1 and MAN 2 enter.

MAN 1: Hello everyone.

MAN 2: We apologise for disturbing you.

CONVINCER: How is that possible?

MAN 1: What, sir?

CONVINCER: That you are here.

MAN 2: Are we not scheduled in the agenda?

CONVINCER: Did you … eh … finish with … your … debts?

MAN 1: It wasn't us. It was the Fire fighter. He threw a bomb into the pub.

CONVINCER: You were not inside?

MAN 2: Not at all. We were doing our tour, conscientiously.

CONVINCER: So, it was only the pub owner that got blown up.

MAN 1: And the fire fighter who threw the bomb. He threw it badly. He went off with it.

THE SAVIOUR: That was foreseen. It was a bomb to go off with.

CONVINCER: And you?

MAN 1: Us? We watched. It was very interesting.

CONVINCER: Something rattles here, but it doesn't matter. We're going with the helicopter and we plant them there.

MAN 2: What helicopter? The one that was trying to land?

CONVINCER: Did you see it? Where is it?

MAN 1: In a hole. Out of service.

CONVINCER: What do you mean?

MAN 1: We were given a gun to shoot at everything that moves. A helicopter moves.

MAN 2: Not anymore. We destroyed it.

CONVINCER: You didn't destroy the helicopter!

MAN 2: It moved. So we fired. The crew members … the motor …

CONVINCER: You destroyed it?

MAN 1: In full flight. Like a duck. It was very amusing.

CONVINCER: Imbeciles!

MAN 2: They always tell us that … always have. We had enough. We're off.

MAN 1: What else can we do here, you ask yourself. No more corpses to transport, no more pub.

THE SAVIOUR: Tell me, you haven't seen … by accident … somewhere … a young girl, who …

MAN 2: Heh … you know, with that fog …

THE SAVIOUR: Is there fog now?

MAN 1: No more moon, no more stars.

MAN 2: We could leave you the gun.

MAN 2 throws the gun at the feet of THE SAVIOUR who picks it up and looks at it. THE SAVED GIRL appears in the back and smiles.

CONVINCER: Where are you two going, you two?

MAN 1: Straight on, over the fields, through the fog.

CONVINCER: On foot?

MAN 2: On foot, barefoot, as usual.

The two men leave. THE SAVIOUR looks at THE SAVED GIRL.

THE SAVED GIRL: Go on … come … come …

THE SAVIOUR: Yes.

> *THE SAVIOUR slowly lifts the gun and shoots himself through the heart. He drops the gun and with arms stretched out, walks towards THE SAVED GIRL. They hug each other.*

CONVINCER: And me?

> *The noise of bulldozers.*

CONVINCER: And the bulldozers are coming!

> *The noise becomes louder and louder.*

CONVINCER: *(Opening the door, screaming into the night.)* Stop! Stop!

> *Crash, black out.*

SAVED GIRL: Good night, the living!

> *End of play.*

THE ATONEMENT

Characters

THE BLIND MAN

THE WIFE

THE DEAF MAN

THE DOCTOR

THE CHILD

THE OLD LADY

THE OTHER BLIND MAN

THE OFFICER

Sequence One

In the flat of the BLIND MAN and his WIFE. A knock on the door.

THE WIFE: Who is there?

THE BLIND MAN: It's me.

THE WIFE: *(Opening the door.)* Already? Couldn't you find shelter somewhere? Wait! Give me your coat! And your hat! Take the snow off your shoes. You'll make everything dirty.

The MAN taps his shoes. The WOMAN shakes the coat and hat of the MAN. She closes the door.

Why did you come home so early?

The MAN throws some change on the table.

Is that all? You could at least have stayed until midnight. It's not that cold.

THE BLIND MAN: *(Sitting down.)* No, not that cold.

THE WIFE: So? *(She chucks the coins in a metal tin and shakes the tin.)* In this tin is all the money you brought in since Tuesday. Do you know how much it is? Do you know? So to speak, nothing. Nothing, do you understand? This cannot go on like this! And, tonight, you allowed yourself to come home even earlier than usual. A Friday evening, when business is a bit better, when people have received their wages, and come out to spend it on the cinema, in the pub, anywhere. And you, you go home just at that moment, because it snows a little, or because your hands were cold.

THE BLIND MAN: No. There was too much noise. Too much screaming.

THE WIFE: Like every Friday evening.

THE BLIND MAN: No. Different. Something else. I heard punches. The screams of an old man. I heard his bones break, his clothes being ripped, his glasses crushed. The soft sound of his fall. His silence …

THE WIFE: It was a fight. A simple fight.

THE BLIND MAN: No. They hit an old man. Several people hit an old defenceless man. I couldn't stay there, listen to it. See it.

THE WIFE: See? You said: See?

THE BLIND MAN: Yes, I saw … coming from his nose, his mouth, his ears, thin red threads forming a dark stain under his head, around his white hair.

THE WIFE: Again. Your attack again.

THE BLIND MAN: The snow is soiled tonight, with enormous pools of blood. On the faces terrible wounds gape open.

THE WIFE: Be quiet! That's enough! Your sedatives! Here! Take this! Quick! Another one! Lay down and try to sleep, poor fool.

Sequence Two

A park in spring. It is sunrise. Birds sing. The BLIND MAN, sitting on a bench, very softly plays the harmonica. A DEAF MAN arrives, his feet crunch on the gravel of the path. He stops before the BLIND MAN and throws a handful of change into the hat, lying on the ground.)

THE BLIND MAN: Thank you.

THE DEAF MAN: You're welcome. They're foreign coins, worthless, that some damn tourists gave me tonight.

THE BLIND MAN: Thank you, anyway.

He starts to play again.

THE DEAF MAN: Don't tier yourself. It's too late, everyone's asleep, there's nobody. And me, I can't hear anything of your music. I'm deaf. *(The BLIND MAN stops playing. Silence.)* Well, say something then. Why don't you say something?

THE BLIND MAN: What's the point … if you are deaf?

THE DEAF MAN: I read lips. If you talk slowly, keep your head turned towards me, I can understand everything you say. Try. Say something.

THE BLIND MAN: You have a nice voice, sir.

THE DEAF MAN: Is that true? I have a nice voice? My voice … I haven't heard it for more than twenty years … But you said that, just to say something.

THE BLIND MAN: I can assure you, sir …

THE DEAF MAN: Stop being so polite and stop saying 'sir'. I'm just a … I'm an artist like you.

THE BLIND MAN: An artist?

THE DEAF MAN: Yes, I'm an artist, even if I'm not a musician. I'm a fire eater. I eat fire, in public places, in the small touristic streets, before pubs, cafes. It is very beautiful. Especially in the evening. That's why I work at night.

THE BLIND MAN: That must be very beautiful.

THE DEAF MAN: It's fantastic! The flames come out of my mouth, like this: Hou hou! They nicknamed me 'The Dragon'. Good hey, for a name, don't you think? The Dragon.

THE BLIND MAN: Yes, that's very nice.

THE DEAF MAN: If you could see me! Even that I'm fifty-six, I'm as strong as a bull. My face is riddled with scars, my eyebrows are burned, my hair scorched. I'm magnificent! I'm a genuine dragon.

THE BLIND MAN: I can imagine it perfectly.

THE DEAF MAN: But I'm also a drunk. I drink everything they give me. I'm soaked with alcohol. One day, there will be an accident. Instead of leaving my mouth, the flames will go back inside, go down my throat, down to my stomach, and I'll explode, like a bomb. Baboum. A living bomb. A bomb of flesh and blood!

Sequence Three

In a hospital.

THE DOCTOR: Take a seat. *(Silence.)* Oh, I'm sorry. You're blind. I didn't know. Your wife didn't tell me. I didn't look at you. Excuse me. Here's a chair.

THE BLIND MAN: *(Sitting down.)* Don't apologise, doctor. You're not supposed to look at everyone who enters your office.

THE DOCTOR: We have been looking for you for three months. We didn't know where to get in touch with you. You left your domicile and …

THE BLIND MAN: I'm here. What do you have to tell me?

THE DOCTOR: Your wife is dying. Did you know that?

THE BLIND MAN: I didn't know. I only hoped so.

THE DOCTOR: Pardon? I must have misunderstood. You hoped so? You didn't say that.

THE BLIND MAN: I did. You heard very well.

THE DOCTOR: How can you … dare you … say that?

THE BLIND MAN: Saying it, is nothing. I think what I say.

THE DOCTOR: You detest her that much?

THE BLIND MAN: That's not the point. Is she suffering?

THE DOCTOR: We are doing everything to ease the suffering.

THE BLIND MAN: That is your profession.

THE DOCTOR: It was also your wife's profession. She was a nurse. *(Silence.)* Would you like to see her?

THE BLIND MAN: See her?

THE DOCTOR: I mean … pay her a visit. Talk to her … one last time. She wants your presence. *(Silence.)* She's worried about you. *(Silence.)* She feels terribly lonely.

THE BLIND MAN: *(Standing up.)* So do I. Can I go now?

THE DOCTOR: *(Also getting up.)* I can't hold you back. And what shall I say to your wife?

THE BLIND MAN: Nothing.

THE DOCTOR: Where can we contact you in case that ...

THE BLIND MAN: Nowhere. I only came to assure myself that she wouldn't get better.

THE DOCTOR: Is there not the tiniest bit of charity or humanity left in you?

THE BLIND MAN: *(Opening the door.)* You better put that question to my wife. Goodbye, doctor.

THE DOCTOR: Tell me ... who has hurt you so much?

THE BLIND MAN: Me? Hurt, me? *(Big laugh.)*

Sequence Four

The BLIND MAN plays in a corridor of the metro. A train arrives, several footsteps ring in the corridor. Brouhaha. A few coins fall into the hat of the BLIND MAN.

THE CHILD: Mum, will you give me a coin for the blind man?

THE MOTHER: Blind? Really! A good-for-nothing! It should not be allowed.

The steps move away.

THE CHILD: Aren't you afraid that someone would steal a coin from your hat?

THE BLIND MAN: No.

THE CHILD: Well, I just took one from you. The biggest one.

THE BLIND MAN: I know. I heard you. It doesn't matter. Keep it. I'm giving it to you.

THE CHILD: I don't want to keep your money. Here. *(He throws the money back into the hat.)* It was just to see if you were really blind. When I grow up, I'll become blind like you, forever. And I will play the harmonica. Or else, I think I'd rather become a gangster. I will attack people in the metro and in the corridors. Banks as well …

THE MOTHER: *(Calling from far away.)* Are you coming or what?

The CHILD runs off. The BLIND MAN starts to play again. Steps of a man stop before him.

THE DEAF MAN: Greetings to you, blind man with the harmonica.

THE BLIND MAN: Greetings, magnificent Dragon.

THE DEAF MAN: Where have you been? I looked for you since the beginning of summer.

THE BLIND MAN: Why?

THE DEAF MAN: To share my bed.

THE BLIND MAN: I don't understand.

THE DEAF MAN: I'll explain it to you. I have a room with a bed at this old lady's place. A room is saying too much, it's just a storage room without a window, but that doesn't matter. I work at night, I sleep during the day. The light would bother me. And you, since you are blind, what good would a window be to you, I wonder.

THE BLIND MAN: It wouldn't.

THE DEAF MAN: You see. On the other hand, the bed would do you, to sleep in. Yours at night, mine during the day.

THE BLIND MAN: The same bed?

THE DEAF MAN: Well, yes, like that, it pays off. She's miserly, the old lady. Kilo can't stand an empty bed laying around all night in a room. Ever since Pinot died, she hasn't stopped harassing me to find someone. Pinot, he'd only one leg. A good bloke. He put wet linen on my forehead when I had drunk too much. He cleaned up my vomit. He was a one of a kind juggler. *(Silence.)* Obviously, if you've got something else …

THE BLIND MAN: I've got nothing else.

THE DEAF MAN: You sleep in parks, under bridges, in the corridors of the metro.

THE BLIND MAN: Yes.

THE DEAF MAN: The cops will pick you up for vagrancy.

THE BLIND MAN: That's already happened.

THE DEAF MAN: Winter's coming. The room isn't heated, but there we're protected from the wind and the snow. There's two thick blankets on the bed. We get hot food, in the Old Lady's kitchen there's always a fire on. *(Silence.)* What did you say?

THE BLIND MAN: Nothing.

THE DEAF MAN: Maybe it disgusts you, to sleep in the same bed as me? That's it, isn't it? I disgust you. I disgust the gentleman. I am too dirty and too disgusting for the gentleman. Well then, that the gentleman permits me to tell him, that he is as dirty and disgusting as I am, if it isn't more! See you later! Farewell, I mean!

THE BLIND MAN: No, that's not it. Don't go, Dragon! Come back! You're right. I'm worse, I'm dirtier, more disgusting than you are.

THE DEAF MAN: No, you're cleaner. I know that I've become repulsive. I used to look after myself, I was intelligent, I spoke well, I wrote well. I was a journalist. It was an explosion, a fucking bomb in a fucking country that made me deaf, half stupid and a complete alcoholic.

THE BLIND MAN: In what country was that?

THE DEAF MAN: I forgot, I can't remember anymore, and I couldn't care less. It was far from here, it happened a long time ago, I forgot everything, everything! I'm very happy being deaf, you know, that way I don't hear the bad sounds. The bad stuff's only in my head. I hear them sometimes though. The shouts, the cries, the explosions ... I hear them.

THE BLIND MAN: And I, sometimes, I see.

Sequence Five

In the OLD LADY's kitchen.

THE OLD LADY: *(Ironic.)* That's original, a blind man who plays the harmonica.

THE DEAF MAN: He plays very well. Much better than the other one. He sings as well. He has a very nice voice.

THE OLD LADY: You heard it, maybe, his voice?

THE DEAF MAN: Of course not. But I looked at the people who were listening to him. They had emotion on their faces.

THE OLD LADY: Emotion! Look at this! It hasn't got the least bit of importance if he plays well or if he plays crap. On the other hand, I'm not having any phonies in my house. Take your glasses off, mister. I recognise a real blind man, at first glance.

THE BLIND MAN: There!

THE DEAF MAN: Fuck me!

THE OLD LADY: What … What happened to your eyes?

THE BLIND MAN: Burned by the sun … torture …

THE DEAF MAN: They've cut his eyelids off.

THE OLD LADY: Anyway, it's not a pretty sight. Put your glasses back on!

THE BLIND MAN: Yes, madam.

THE OLD LADY: You, Dragon, go to bed, and sleep it off. I'll take care of the gentleman.

THE DEAF MAN: So, we'll keep him. Till tonight, my poor old man. *(He goes.)*

THE OLD LADY: Give me your jacket.

THE BLIND MAN: Why?

THE OLD LADY: Here one obeys, without asking questions. Everyone obeys me. I have six lodgers. What would happen, if everyone just did whatever came into their heads? So, your jacket.

THE BLIND MAN: Here you go, madam.

THE OLD LADY: It's still in pretty good nick. Could sell this. I'll give you another one, not as nice, when it gets really cold. You shouldn't be too well dressed for begging. The clothes as well should evoke pity.

THE BLIND MAN: I'm not looking for pity.

THE OLD LADY: I know, I know. You're all artists! Only, artist or beggar, I don't see the difference. The only one who works here, is me. Who took care of you up till now?

THE BLIND MAN: My wife. She died in spring.

THE OLD LADY: May God have her soul. But then, the dead don't have worries anymore. Unlike us … Here you'll be fine. You'll have a room, a bed. In the evening, I give you a full meal with bread. The police knows who I am. You'll have no problem from that side either. When I busy myself with someone, he can be as calm as he was in his mother's belly. Come!

THE BLIND MAN: Where are we going?

THE OLD LADY: Out, on the street. I know the good corners for playing music. In the evening, I come look for you. When they give you food, you can eat it. Money, on the other hand, you give to me. All the money! And no trickery! I will search you. When you had a good day, I will give you something. Do you drink?

THE BLIND MAN: No, madam.

THE OLD LADY: Do you smoke?

THE BLIND MAN: No, madam.

THE OLD LADY: Then you don't need any money at all.

Sequence Six

Before the house of the OLD LADY. Sound of traffic.

THE DEAF MAN: So, your first day at work? The Old Lady happy with you?

THE BLIND MAN: I don't know. She didn't say anything.

THE DEAF MAN: That means she is happy. Otherwise, you would have heard.

THE BLIND MAN: There's a strange sound I'm hearing. As if they're tapping on a pot with a metal spoon.

THE DEAF MAN: It time for soup. We're going to eat, come.

THE BLIND MAN: A piece of bread and a glass of water is enough for me. I don't feel like a full meal.

THE DEAF MAN: Well, it has all you need. It's an immense cauldron of soup, made with all sorts of rotten vegetables that the Old Lady gathers at the market and with scraps of meat that she buys for her cats.

THE BLIND MAN: She has cats?

THE DEAF MAN: That's us, her cats.

THE BLIND MAN: Tell me, Dragon, the other lodgers, who are they?

THE DEAF MAN: People like us. Low lives. A one arm, an idiot, one without legs and another blind guy. I'll introduce you. Come.

THE BLIND MAN: What happened to him, the blind man?

THE DEAF MAN: Nothing. He was born like that. Follow me.

They enter the kitchen. Sound of dishes, voices.

THE DEAF MAN: Good day, artists! I present to you a new friend. He's blind.

A VOICE: And he plays the harmonica?

THE DEAF MAN: Of course. Sit here, next to me. It was Pinot's place.

VOICE 1: Are there no more bits of meat? I would like a few more bits of meat.

THE OLD LADY: Everyone would like a few more bits of meat.

VOICE 2: Here, eat mine, it disgusts me. It stinks.

THE OLD LADY: It stinks because you haven't got any teeth left. It disgusts you because you can't chew them, those bits of meat. The truth is that you're dying for them.

VOICE 1: Me too, I am dying for them. I never have enough meat. Only liquor and cabbage.

THE OLD LADY: You just have to dunk your bread in the liquor. Are you not eating your soup, sir? Does it not become you?

THE BLIND MAN: It does, madam. But I have taken the habit of eating nothing but dry bread.

THE OLD LADY: Oh well, I will have you change your habits. I insist that my boarders eat properly. So they are well nourished. Vitamins, proteins, all that. Otherwise they become ill. And who will pay for the pharmacy, the doctor, the burial? Me, maybe? And with what, if you please?

THE OTHER BLIND MAN: Say, Sir, I'd like to know. Have you always been blind, like me?

THE BLIND MAN: No. Only for a couple of years. You're very young, according to your voice.

THE OTHER BLIND MAN: I was never young. I am twenty-seven. It's long life, very long. It will never stop. If at least I knew what colours are. Colours, you have seen them. Explain them to me, please.

VOICE 1: He's starting again!

VOICE 2: It will make him go mental, colours.

THE BLIND MAN: I'm sorry. Colours are inexplicable, unimaginable when you are blind from birth. But don't regret it. What you know is the absence of colour, black. The opposite of black is white. White holds all the other colours. It hurts, it burns. It makes you scream with pain.

Sequence Seven

Very early in the morning. The DEAF MAN, very drunk, arrives in the room. The noise of furniture being overthrown.

THE BLIND MAN: What is going on? Is it six o'clock already?

THE DEAF MAN: I think I made some noise. Where's my pocket light? There. Put your glasses on, good God, you're a real nightmare! I woke you up, I'm sorry. I'm a bit drunk. Don't get up. Stay in bed. It's only three or four o'clock. I'll finish my bottle quietly while waiting.

THE BLIND MAN: *(Getting up.)* I'm not tired anymore.

THE DEAF MAN: You have the right to sleep until six o'clock. You have the right to stay in bed. Go back to sleep.

THE BLIND MAN: Don't argue. Take the bed. You're numb with cold.

THE DEAF MAN: What did you say?

THE BLIND MAN: Your hands are frozen. Go to sleep. I'll take your shoes off.

THE DEAF MAN: *(Falling on the bed.)* It's so cold, good God! It's freezing outside. I fell four or five times on my way home, so slippery. It's very nice in a bed warmed up before hand! Thanks. You're a good man. Yes. For a long time I wanted to tell you ...

THE BLIND MAN: What?

THE DEAF MAN: The truth about me. I lied to you. But now I will tell you the truth, and you'll be the only one to know.

THE BLIND MAN: No, no, please! Tomorrow. Now sleep.

THE DEAF MAN: No. Right now. Tomorrow I won't have the courage for it anymore. But I will switch of my lamp first. If I don't see you anymore, you cannot interrupt me. There you go. What I told you about the bomb, about the explosion, those were lies. Those damn bombs in those damn countries, it was me who set them off. I never was a journalist. I was what they call an anarchist, a terrorist. The

last bomb … I went off with it. Sadly, it didn't kill me. I
had wounds all over my body and face, but I wasn't dead.
Others died. I saw them fall. I saw the blood, the disfigured
faces, the twisted bodies. Those that weren't dead had
their mouths wide open. They screamed and I, I couldn't
hear a thing. I saw them run, scream, die, but I didn't hear
them. My eardrums were gone. It was like in a nightmare.
(Silence.) They took me for a victim of the explosion, they
treated me. My wounds healed, but my soul never will. I'm
deaf, but my head is filled with explosions, with cries, with
groans, with tears. Impossible to forget. I am and I always
will be the lowest of the human beings, an executioner,
an assassin, a piece of filth. *(Silence, then with a sob.)* There
were children as well, imagine, children …

The sobs, slowly, turn into snoring.

THE BLIND MAN: If you are a piece of filth, then what am I?
Torture is of a monstrous lowness, more despicable then
murder. I'm a torturer. For years, by order of my superiors,
helped by my wife, I tortured defenceless beings. Guilty or
innocent, it mattered little to us, we only had contempt for
our victims. My wife and I, we found a deep satisfaction in
our hideous work, a certain pleasure even. This aberration
lasted up to the day when one of our colleagues filmed
us during a torture session. When I saw, on screen, this
shameful scene of which I was the principle character, I
saw myself for the first time as I really was, what I really
was. Incapable to bare the sight of my demeaning, of my
degradation, I ran off before the end of the film. Of course
they went looking for me and found me a few days later. A
few weeks later, sitting in the office of an officer, I waited
indifferently for the arrival of my wife and the verdict of
our superiors.

Sequence Eight

In the OFFICER's office.

THE OFFICER: Your husband, Madame.

THE WIFE: Where is he? It's not ... this man?

THE OFFICER: It's him, alright.

THE WIFE: That's impossible! What happened to him? Why
    is he wearing dark glasses? Why is he in this state? What
    have you done to him?

THE OFFICER: We? How dare you insinuate! ... Calm yourself,
    Madame. We found your husband after a five day search.

THE WIFE: Why didn't you notify me right away?

THE OFFICER: We had to fix him up first, then interrogate him,
    and make a decision about your case.

THE WIFE: But what happened to him? Why did he flee?
    Where was he? What did he do?

THE OFFICER: We found him by the sea, slumped on the sand,
    in a semi-conscious state. He hadn't eaten, or drunk for five
    days, on top of that, his eyelids were cut off, and his eyes
    completely burned by the sun.

THE WIFE: Oh no. Who did that to him?

THE OFFICER: He inflicted this mutilation on himself.

THE BLIND MAN: I have inflicted it upon so many others ...
    I stared at the sun at its zenith until all became darkness.
    Total darkness, everywhere, forever.

THE WIFE: Why? Why did you do this?

THE BLIND MAN: To make up for our crimes. Death seemed
    too easy, too quick.

THE WIFE: What are you saying? What crimes?

THE BLIND MAN: I didn't want to anymore. From that moment
    on I couldn't look in the mirror anymore. I couldn't look at
    my hands again, I couldn't look at you again, you.

THE WIFE: Me, I don't understand. What's wrong with me?

THE BLIND MAN: You are completely covered in blood.

THE WIFE: He is mad, isn't he?

THE OFFICER: He is, his mind is disturbed. Therefore, in the interest of everyone, we thought it would be desirable that you left the country for good. Your trip has already been organised.

THE WIFE: Where are we going?

THE OFFICER: You will know at the airport. We'll drive you there in a few hours. At the arrival, people you can trust will be waiting for you. You will easily find work because of your nursing qualifications. About him, you'll have to see. His sight is gone forever, but for the rest ... Maybe he will recover over time.

Sequence Nine

THE BLIND MAN: I didn't 'recover' over time. Thoughts of my shameful past, intolerable visions haunted me. My wife, on the other hand, never felt the least remorse.

THE WIFE: *(Offstage Voice.)* I had enough! Stop tormenting yourself, stop tormenting me! We are not responsible ... We only obeyed orders ... We were helping a cause ... It was a job as another ... Someone had to do it ... We weren't the only ones doing it ... Elsewhere they torture as well ... There's torture all over the world ...

THE BLIND MAN: All over the world torturers try to justify themselves like this. But no order, no cause will excuse our crimes. For them pardon, and oblivion does not exist. That blemish cannot be wiped from our souls, not by death, not by atonement.

End of play.

LINE, THE TIME

Characters

LINE, 12 years old

MARC, 22 years old

LINE, 22 years old

MARC, 32 years old

Part One

The dialogue, in the two parts, could be interspersed with or accompanied by different sounds: an ice cream vendor passing, calling out: 'Vanilla, chocolate!' a barrel organ, calls, shouts and the crying of several children, etc.

LINE: *(Calling.)* See you tomorrow, Valentine! *(She stops before MARC.)* Marc? Are you sad?

MARC: Hello, Line.

LINE: She didn't come?

MARC: Who? No, she came. But she was in a hurry.

LINE: She's always in a hurry.

MARC: Because of children. Because of her employers.

LINE: The other young girls are never in a hurry. Yesterday, I saw Annette, who talked for an hour with a guy with a beard.

MARC: Annette, she talks to anyone.

LINE: Because she is nice. And because she's not in a hurry.

MARC: Go and play, Line.

LINE: I can't play anymore, I have to go home. It is almost evening.

MARC: Then you have to go home.

LINE: Oh, I still have time to talk a little bit with you.

MARC: I don't feel like talking, Line. I would like to be alone.

LINE: Am I bothering you?

MARC: You're not bothering me, but … you can't understand.

LINE: I do, I understand. You are sad, because she was in a hurry.

MARC: No. Not because she was in a hurry, because she acted as if she was in a hurry.

LINE: She doesn't feel like stopping when she sees you, that's all. She doesn't want to talk to you. You don't please her. You don't interest her.

MARC: What are you poking your nose in for? And first, wipe your mouth.

LINE: Why? Do I have a moustache? I just had a caramel ice cream.

MARC: I can see that.

LINE: *(Wiping her mouth.)* Can you still see it?

MARC: Yes, a little, a tiny bit. Do you brush your hair sometimes?

LINE: Every morning. Why?

MARC: You wouldn't say.

LINE: Obviously, by the evening … and you? Why are you dressed like that?

MARC: I am dressed … normal.

LINE: No, not normal. You are wearing a scarf. It's too hot to be wearing a scarf. I'm on my bare feet, and I'm not cold.

MARC: I didn't put the scarf on because it's cold. I put it on to look good.

LINE: You think that looks good, a scarf? *(Stressing the 'p'.)* It's not because your papa can speak Spanish that he has to purchase his prince a purple poncho.

MARC: Line, you are spitting on me.

LINE: Exactly, it's that what's funny.

MARC: That's not funny.

LINE: It is. We invented that with Valentine. Each time a girl from class tries to show off with her dress or something, we tell her that and we spit on her. It's not because your p …

MARC: Will you stop immediately, Line! You can be so annoying.

LINE: It's not nice of you to say that to me, Marc. I just wanted to make you laugh. But you don't understand jokes. And also, I like you better without your scarf. You have a beautiful bronzed neck.

MARC: Come on, Line!

LINE: Yes, I think so. Why do you do all that, Marc?

MARC: Do what?

LINE: You dress like a scarecrow, you blush when she walks by, you act all stupid.

MARC: Are you spying on me?

LINE: No, I see you through the bushes. And I don't like it when you are not like … like how you usually are.

MARC: You can't understand. I do all that simply so she would like me.

LINE: Why is that so important, that she likes you?

MARC: You, little Line. Don't you like it when people like you?

LINE: I don't know. I don't think I really care. If they like me, so much the better. If they don't like me, so much the worse.

MARC: You don't say 'so much the worse', you say too bad.

LINE: Too bad, then.

MARC: But that's surely not all the same to you.

LINE: Of course, I like more if …

MARC: I prefer …

LINE: Yes, I prefer it if they like me, but as I am, like that.

MARC: Your parents.

LINE: My parents don't have anything to do with it. My parents love me anyway. But the love of my parents that is not my future.

MARC: Well then! Your future! So young!

LINE: I am not that young! I am twelve, I am only ten years younger than you.

MARC: That's a lot, ten years, Line that is enormous.

LINE: Ten years is nothing. I asked Mum. My dad is eight years older than she is, so?

MARC: What do you mean, Line?

LINE: Nothing. *(Pause.)* But I think that you shouldn't.

MARC: What shouldn't I?

LINE: Show yourself different than you are, to please.

MARC: You can't understand, Line. You are just a little girl.

LINE: Yes, a little girl that plays barefoot on the street. But I'll grow, very quick. The years go by very quickly, don't you know? One day follows another and ... And then I will be a big girl.

MARC: Of course, one day you will be a big girl.

LINE: Big enough to get married.

MARC: To get married? It's too soon to think about that, Line.

LINE: Nevertheless, I'm already thinking about it. And I will tell you Marc, I will marry nobody else but you.

MARC: Nobody else but me? And why?

LINE: Because you are beautiful, because you taught me how to play chess and because I love you.

MARC: You love me as a good friend, Line.

LINE: Yes, but much more. I love you like mum or dad, but much more, just like my friend Valentine, but even more, like my cat Charabia, and still more. I am completely in love with you.

MARC: Listen, Line! You don't say things like that.

LINE: Why? I am telling you, it's true. I know you shouldn't tell lies, that, I understand, and I don't tell them very often. But the truth. You can always tell the truth, no? And it's really true that I am in love with you.

MARC: Line, you don't even know what that is. It's not of your age.

LINE: My age! Always my age! Well, I'm ahead of my age. I know very well what it is to be in love. It's when you want to marry someone.

MARC: Not always, Line. Not necessarily.

LINE: Oh, not immediately. I'm not that stupid. But in five
  years, eight years …

MARC: In five years, in eight years, you won't be thinking of
  me anymore, Line.

LINE: Now there you are mistaken. It's you who doesn't know
  what love is.

MARC: I would really like to know nothing about it at all.

LINE: Why? It's so beautiful. In the evening I think of you. I
  imagine you sitting on the side of my bed. You smile at me.
  Then, I fall asleep.

And when I wake up, I'm happy. I run into the park to find
  you. If I wasn't in love with you, what would I do?

MARC: You would go to school. You would play with
  Valentine.

LINE: Yes. But what would I think about? Who would I dream
  about? No, if you didn't exist, Marc, it would be like …
  like when it rains.

MARC: Love isn't always happiness, Line. It makes you suffer
  as well.

LINE: I know that. You don't think that it hurts me to see you
  sitting here, stupidly, waiting for a young girl that doesn't
  even look at you? And I can tell you that you disgust me
  with your scarf and your good manners. I almost want to
  be in love with someone else, when I see you like that.

MARC: Yes, that would be better. Be in love with someone else,
  Line. With a boy of your age.

LINE: With a boy of my age? Have you already seen a boy
  of my age? They do nothing but annoy us during class,
  and then, they play go and play football. Anyway, do you
  believe, Marc that we can choose? Choose who we love?

MARC: No, we can't, you are right. But … are you crying?
  Don't cry little Line, come now, don't cry.

LINE: I'm not crying, I'm fuming. You'll see. Soon I'll be
  big. And I'll be more beautiful than her, and much more

intelligent, and much nicer, and I will never be in a hurry, you'll see, in five or eight years, you'll see.

MARC: Yes, Line, don't cry, easy now, go home. Listen, it's your mum calling you.

MOTHER: Line! Line! Come home immediately! It's gone past eight.

LINE: Yes, Mum. I'm coming! I'm looking for the cat. *(She goes, shouting.)* Charabia! Charabia!

Part Two

Ten years later. The same park. LINE sits on a bench. She is reading.
MARC walks by.

LINE: Marc!

MARC: *(Stops.)* Miss?

LINE: Marc, don't you recognise me?

MARC: I'm sorry, I don't see …

LINE: Marc! It's me, Line.

MARC: Line? No, that's impossible! I had a little neighbour
called Line …

LINE: Time passes, Marc. I'm twenty-two.

MARC: Twenty-two! I never would have recognised you.
You've changed a lot.

LINE: You see, I recognised you immediately. You haven't
changed that much. But you have become much older.

MARC: Don't exaggerate, Line. I'm only thirty-two. But can I
just talk to you, still, I mean, again?

LINE: Yes, still and again. You want to sit down for a moment?

MARC: *(Sitting down.)* Yes, if you don't mind. *(Pause.)*

LINE: Why did you come back after so many years?

MARC: Why? Maybe to find a little girl that played with a hoop.

LINE: The hula-hoop is passé.

MARC: What do children play with then these days?

LINE: I don't know. It changes all the time.

MARC: And you Line, what do you play with now?

LINE: I don't play anymore. I read. I study economics.

MARC: Economics? You?

LINE: Yes, me. Why does that surprise you?

MARC: I don't know. It's true. Why wouldn't you study
economics?

LINE: You seem sad, Marc. Is it because of my studies?

MARC: No. Not just that. It's also because of your hair.

LINE: What's with my hair?

MARC: It's shorter, and it's nicely done.

LINE: When there's no wind, it's nice.

MARC: While ... before ... It was never nicely done. And your mouth, and your feet ...

LINE: My mouth and my feet?

MARC: Your mouth is not smeared with chocolate, and you're wearing shoes, Line. You're not barefoot.

LINE: *(Laughing.)* And you haven't got that scarf, Marc.

MARC: What scarf?

LINE: That scarf you put on when you tried to please a certain person.

MARC: You didn't like my scarf, I remember. You liked my bare tanned neck.

LINE: Now don't be rude, Marc. *(Pause.)* Where have you been for so long?

MARC: I was in England. I followed a woman there.

LINE: Was she always in a hurry?

MARC: Not really. I even had the time to marry her.

LINE: Congratulations.

MARC: Thanks! I'm divorced now.

LINE: Bravo!

MARC: You're making fun of me.

LINE: Why not? I find it all very funny.

MARC: Line!

LINE: Everyone calls me Caroline now. Line is just a cute name you give to children. My real name is Caroline.

MARC: To me you'll always be Line. Line, if I came back, it's because of you.

LINE: You came back for a little girl who so desperately loved you?

MARC: Did you love me, Line? Really?

LINE: I even told you once. I loved your hair, your eyes, your arm, your bronzed neck, your shyness, your sweetness, I loved every bit of you, Marc, and … you left.

MARC: I came back.

LINE: You didn't come back for me. You came back to find the atmosphere of the past, your youth, your dreams, your illusions.

MARC: And the little girl that loved me. That was you, Line.

LINE: It was. Anyway, you're too old for me, Marc.

MARC: Ten years of difference, that's nothing.

LINE: My parents had eight years of difference. They divorced.

MARC: They didn't divorce necessarily because of their age difference.

LINE: No, not necessarily. You are divorced, you too, and there wasn't a great age difference between you two, am I right?

MARC: Almost none. Barely a year.

LINE: Why did you divorce, Marc?

MARC: Oh, Line. I don't know. Time passes, people change … It's too difficult to explain.

LINE: And I'm still too young to understand, no doubt.

MARC: In one sense, yes. You don't have the experience of marriage.

LINE: Except for the experience of my parent's marriage. Did you have children, Marc?

MARC: No. No, children, luckily.

LINE: Yes, luckily.

MARC: You still live around here, Line?

LINE: No, I don't. I have a room on the college grounds, but I come to visit my mother from time to time.

MARC: My mother, she died.

LINE: I know. I went to her funeral. You weren't there.

MARC: It was just at a time of my life when ... I couldn't come. But I went to see her grave this morning.

LINE: Yes. *(Pause.)* And what are you thinking of doing now?

MARC: I don't know. Find work ...

LINE: What sort of work? You gave up your studies because of her.

Mark: Any work, just enough to live. I'd like to stay around here, find a room ...

LINE: Any work! Find a room! If you hadn't left ...

MARC: Don't get angry.

LINE: Get angry? Why? *(Pause.)*

MARC: Line?

LINE: Caroline!

MARC: To me, Line. Always.

LINE: Caroline, to everyone.

MARC: I'm not everyone. You loved me.

LINE: Ten years ago.

MARC: Yes, time ...

LINE: Yes, time. I don't know your past, Marc. Your ten years passed by away from me. And you, you don't know my past.

MARC: You haven't got a past yet. You are so young.

LINE: I am young, yes, but I have a past: you. For ten years I came into this park, every day. You weren't there anymore, the park was there, full of children, mothers, young girls, old men. Full of people and somehow, empty. Without you, for me, it was a desert.

MARC: I couldn't know it was ... serious. A little girl, twelve years old ... But now I am here, Line, and you're not a child anymore.

LINE: You are here, yes. The sun should come up, the days should light up, but nothing happens.

MARC: We could maybe find each other again … begin again … everything.

LINE: We can't hide those ten years, Marc. I dreamed a lot about you and about your return, you know? But in my dreams, it was different. You were bigger, more beautiful, happier. You came back to find me, but you didn't have that sad and heavy past on your shoulders. Oh, Marc! I believed I would never see you again! *(She gets up. MARC takes her arm.)*

MARC: You don't leave me any hope?

LINE: Did you leave me any? Let go of my arm, will you! By the way I'm very busy. I have exams in three weeks.

LINE goes. A YOUNG GIRL enters, running on bare feet. She should have the same voice as the young LINE.

YOUNG GIRL: Goodbye Jeanne, see you tomorrow! *(She stops in front of MARC, who has sat down again on the bench.)* Are you sad, sir?

MARC: What did you say?

YOUNG GIRL: I asked if you were sad because she left.

MARC: Who?

YOUNG GIRL: The lady.

MARC: What lady? It was a young girl, not a lady.

YOUNG GIRL: She looks like a lady. She wears high heels.

MARC: Young girls wear high heels too.

YOUNG GIRL: Do you mean, high heels also wear young girls? It's more logical.

MARC: Yes, you're right, Line. It is more logical.

YOUNG GIRL: My name is not Line. It's Aline.

MARC: Aline? Well. That's beautiful.

YOUNG GIRL: They also call me Mandolin, Crinoline, Air-line, and all that. You're not going to give me a stupid name like that, are you?

MARC: Line is not a stupid name.

YOUNG GIRL: But that's not my name. I like more …

MARC: I prefer. You say: I prefer.

YOUNG GIRL: You talk like a teacher. *(MARC gets up.)* Where are you going? *(MARC starts running.)*

(Shouting.) I know her, you know. I see her every day. It's useless running after her. She never talks to anyone and she's always in a hurry.

MARK's steps.

End of play.

Afterword

As is probably the story with most of her readers, *The Notebook* was the first work of fiction I read of Ágota Kristóf. When I opened the book, I had no idea what I was about to encounter. When I closed it again, a few dense hours later, I was dumbfounded, stunned as one is, after been given a lesson in brutal honesty and simplicity. It felt like a slap, I can't really remember where, or the back of my head, or on my bare bottom.

So I went looking for more. Not immediately available, I ordered the rest of the trilogy online. *The Illiterate*, a personal account of her writing, I did find in the bookshop and read next, while I was waiting for the rest of the trilogy to arrive. In *The Illiterate* she mentions writing for theatre, plays. Again I went looking. Not only was it not to be found in any bookshop in London or on Amazon, it wasn't available in English, at all. Once more I went online, Amazon.fr, this time and, miraculously, a few days later, I started to read the first of her plays.

So, unlike most of her readers, this is what Ágota Kristóf became to me: *The Notebook* and that very first play: *John and Joe*.

I should mention that I am fascinated by theatre. Not so much by the performance element, as by its slightly forgotten, if not ignored, literary merit, its possibilities. Whenever a writer catches my eye, I tend to look for the dramatic works.

I should also mention that at the time, I was translating *Fando and Lis*, that brilliant, but sadly forgotten play by Fernando Arrabal. His similar brutal honesty, as it felt at the time, had too much in common with *The Notebook*, not to feel a serious shiver in the back of my spine, when I opened up the first page towards the first lines of *John and Joe*. I was prepared to be shocked. And shocked I was indeed.

But I wasn't prepared for this: *John and Joe* is a meandering, (do I dare say:) funny dialogue between two old poor bums who end up arguing over how to pay the bill at a bar. As a result, the meagre winnings of a lottery ticket fall in the hands of the wrong man. There is a small fight and one of them ends up in prison for the night. The next day amendments are made. The play does not so much end as open up to a repeat of that same minimal moment of drama.

No. I wasn't disappointed. I just read a very good play. I knew I had just read a very good play. It just wasn't what I was expecting. Where was that *violence*, in any of its forms? Where was that brutal honesty?

The only physical violence present in *John and Joe* is a light scuffle between the two main characters with the very clear stage directions by Ágota Kristóf herself: *They tug each other, without hitting one another*. Really?

I was confused. I just couldn't understand. Did she write this? Did the same writer who wrote *The Notebook* write *John and Joe*?

To come in any way to an answer to this question, I should turn it around. Ágota Kristóf wrote *John and Joe* in 1972, *The Notebook* in 1986. It changes the question. How did she get from *John and Joe* to *The Notebook*?

Looking at the other plays she wrote (most of these predate *The Notebook*) doesn't really help. All the other plays show her brutal view of the world. She is rather unforgiving. Seventeen named characters are brutally killed within nine plays (no one dies in *John and Joe*, so that makes it eight plays). A further 500 or so (probably more: two whole villages, one public bombing, the victims of a professional torturer over a long period of time and those of a government official) are killed during the play, or in direct relation to the storylines. That is not bad going if you consider the word count: 46,311 in this translation, which comes roughly down to about one character each page, or should we say, one a day ... Maybe that is not such a shocking number. Maybe it depends on which part of the world you live in, or came from ...

Is *John and Joe* than such a one-off? Something she wrote on a good day, or a bad day, whichever way you look at it? No. This is clearly Ágota Kristóf's work. For one thing, a lot of the quirkiness and tenderness you find in *John and Joe*, you also find in her other plays: a few quotes should suffice.

The Atonement:

THE OLD WOMAN: [...] When they give you food, you can eat it. Money on the other hand, you give to me, All the money! [...] Do you drink?

THE BLIND MAN: No, madam.

THE OLD WOMAN: Do you smoke?

THE BLIND MAN: No, madam.

THE OLD WOMAN: Then you need no money at all.

The Lift Key:

THE WOMAN: But what a beautiful thing the wait, when you are sure ... [*Wild, she turns to the audience.*] Of what? Sure of what then? [*Shaking her head.*] Sure ... of the return of ... the loved one.

The Grey Hour:

SHE: Do you realise, if you were dead, they wouldn't even let me know.

Line, the Time:

LINE: My age! Always my age! Well, I'm ahead of my age. I know very well what it is to be in love. It's when you want to marry someone.

So, once again, how does *John and Joe* fit in? How does it relate to *The Notebook*? Maybe the answer lies in the title: *John and Joe.* That is two people.

Within all her plays, there is no such thing as a single person, a person on his own, alone. That simply does not exist. If for any reason one of her characters does end up alone, (being abandoned, or separating oneself) it means death, immediate or long coming (*The Monster, The Atonement, The Lift key, The Grey Hour*). Twins, to reach out straight to *The Notebook,* are myriad in all its variations. (The two Firemen and the two Men in *The Epidemic.* The Blind Man in *The Atonement* replaces another Blind Man in the homeless shelter, who used to play the harmonica just like him. Later, the Blind Man is confronted by a man, born blind, unlike him.) Personalities are split up into two separate characters on stage (*A Passing Rat, The Epidemic*). Or they are split up in real and fictional characters (*The Lift Key, The Epidemic, The Road*). The contrast or conflict between two people is constantly played out: Male-female, happy-unhappy, age difference. (Interestingly played out in *Line, the Time.*) Then there is attraction-repulsion and the forced relationship. (*John and Joe, The Grey Hour The Lift Key.*) The 'love' relationship is present throughout.

That constant relationship/conflict between people, played out in between truth, lies and fiction, underlines everything in Ágota Kristóf's work. All coming from her own experience of duality and conflict, fleeing war and death, exiled into a foreign country, a foreign culture, having to speak a language not her own, one she even disliked but was forced to use, to do what she loved best: write.

And so, she wrote *John and Joe*. Let us look at it again.

The two characters that make up this play/are this play, exist only in the conflict that is between them; a conflict that ultimately separates them. They are forced to resolve it, to avoid separation and thus annihilation. But then, as soon as they are back together, they rekindle the conflict, to be able to continue their existence. (Writing this feels like describing the surprisingly complex life pattern of two single celled organisms living in a tiny pool of murky water. I am probably not far off.) It is the elements of need and love between the two characters, that move things along, make for continuation.

Written years later, *The Notebook* reads like a distillation of this play. Here the elements of need/love and conflict between the two main characters have been filtered out, creating a strong bond between the two, and creating the possibility of a search, not for love but for 'true' knowledge, unburdened by the need/love element. The bond is rather extreme:

When the father wants to separate the twins to go to different classes in school, believing it to be a good thing. The mother says:

No, never. I know. I know them. They are one and the same person.

When the father does separate them, within a few hours, they simply lose consciousness, cease to be. (You recognise this.)

With the Twins now an entity, the focus moves from the conflict between two characters to that between the Twins and the world around them.

The Twins handle that conflict with their irrevocable logic, void of need/love. It is that same logic that makes their bond so strong, steers their search, but here also allows for that whisper of aggression in *John and Joe* to turn into the extreme violence we are all too familiar with. The reason behind that logic, is as much a reaction against the world they live in, (one of abandonment, war and violence, the only world they know) as it is a copy of it.

The need/love in this world is replaced by a hankering, a longing, that can only be resolved by the act of making love, debased into a pure physical act, a sensation perceived rather than received and where the other involved (willingly or not) has no meaning, is but a tool and replaced at will. The twins partake, but never allow it to overtake as the driving force of their existence, as it seems to be for most of the people around them.

And so, they survive that world, continue their search, continue their logic, and come to their last, ultimate act of violence: their own willing separation, their own annihilation in Ágota Kristóf's world, (something she valued as requisite to a writer) and so they open up a new search and maybe a new understanding, explored in the rest of the trilogy.

It seems the distillation has gone as far as it can go and has moved away as far as possible from *John and Joe*. But *John and Joe* has not been filtered out completely. It is *The Notebook*'s irrevocable logic, allowing extreme brutal violence, guiding the search for 'true' knowledge that also irrevocably results in moments of tenderness, in kindness; moments that, just as in *John and Joe*, allow life to continue.

Reading *John and Joe* next to *The Notebook* is an experience few authors can offer. These two works of fiction from one and the same hand, that seem to deny, annul and fight each other, while they are each other's counterpart, are each other's consequence, each other's filter and ultimately, do the same thing, look for the same thing, that same old thing we all are looking for, if only we knew how.

Bart Smet, May 2018